# MIKA

Alan Henry is the Grand Prix Editor of the seminal weekly magazine, *Autocar*, and of the *Guardian* newspaper. He has covered Formula 1 since the early 1970s, which places him in a unique position among motoring writers as someone who has witnessed the development of Formula 1 in the modern age. A prolific author, his recent works include a biography of the 1996 World Champion, Damon Hill and a study of legendary Formula 1 drivers entitled *Racers*. The latter book was also published by Queensgate.

# MIKA

## ALAN HENRY

Q

QUEENSGATE PUBLICATIONS

First published in 2000
by Queensgate Publications
Cookham, Berkshire

© Queensgate Securities Ltd, 2000
Text © Alan Henry, 2000

ISBN 1-902655-26-5

A catalogue record of this book is available from the British Library

Photographs by Formula 1 Pictures
Cover design by Charlie Webster
Book design by Production Line, Minster Lovell, Oxford
Production by Landmark Consultants, Princes Risborough,
Buckinghamshire
Printed in England by Cox & Wyman

# Contents

# Introduction

# The gentle Finn with the sheepish grin

Two Sundays at Suzuka, a year apart. On both occasions the sun shone down from a cloudless sky. On both occasions a scarlet Ferrari driven by Michael Schumacher was on pole position. On both occasions he shared the front row with Mika Häkkinen's gleaming silver McLaren–Mercedes. And on both occasions the gentle Finn with the sheepish grin finished the afternoon as the World Champion.

It had taken 96 attempts for the young man to win his first Grand Prix. He posted that maiden victory in the 1997 European Grand Prix at Jeréz in Spain – a race made famous by the controversial collision between Jacques Villeneuve's Williams and Schumacher's Ferrari which resolved the title battle in favour of the free-spirited Canadian driver. The events of that afternoon also resulted in Schumacher having his second place in the Championship officially annulled by motor racing's governing body, the FIA.

Almost unnoticed amid the furore which surrounded these convoluted events, the race was also a psychologically crucial turning point for Häkkinen. Throughout 1997 he had been partnered by the British driver David Coulthard, who had arrived in the McLaren line-up at the start of the previous year. The young Scot had already won the 1995 Portuguese Grand Prix at the wheel of a Williams and therefore joined McLaren with something of a mental advantage over Mika; an apparent edge consolidated with Coulthard's further wins in the 1997 Australian and Italian Grands Prix. It seemed as though the Scot was gaining the upper hand.

The Häkkinen/Coulthard pairing at McLaren threw into stark relief the complexities of life for two drivers of ostensibly similar calibre in a top-line Grand Prix racing team. As a sporting spectacle Formula One can be said to be unique in many respects, not least for the way in which it throws team-mates together as potentially bitter enemies. On the one hand an F1 team is a single cohesive unit, melded together with the single purpose of defeating the opposition. Yet the obvious paradox is that the rivalry between team-mates is always the most intensely fought battle of all. Häkkinen in a McLaren versus Villeneuve, Damon Hill, Heinz-Harald Frentzen, or whomever, in a Williams, is one thing. All sorts of intangibles cloud the equation. How good is one car compared to the other in specific conditions? It is a difficult call. Yet between team-mates the challenge is more starkly delineated. To all intents and purposes, their cars are the same. Clearly the man who wins the most races is the better driver of the two. Obvious, isn't it?

If Häkkinen felt slightly beleaguered in the late summer of 1997, he had every right to be. Success after success seemed to be slipping through his fingers. At Silverstone, prior to qualifying for that year's British Grand Prix, McLaren's Managing Director Ron Dennis professed such confidence in Häkkinen's potential that he staked £2,000 – at odds of

10–1, as I recall – on the Finn finally breaking his F1 duck. With just over six laps left to run, Häkkinen was leading by a couple of lengths from Villeneuve's Williams. The author, who had taken a leaf out of Dennis's book and placed a similar bet – admittedly, for a more modest outlay – was mentally counting his winnings when Mika's engine expired. Villeneuve inherited the win and the disconsolate Häkkinen began the long walk back to the pits.

Häkkinen would tap further into that deep vein of disappointment at Monza, where he was the fastest car on the track for much of the Italian Grand Prix. Unfortunately a tyre failure intervened and he had to be content with ninth place on a day when David took the top spot on the podium.

For Ron Dennis and the McLaren management, Mika's dilemma was clear for all to see. He had all the requisite raw materials at his disposal, but still had to work out the personal formula whereby he unlocked the door to his first win. This in itself raises another fascinating point. Winning one's first Grand Prix has always proved to be a more than usually demanding challenge. Yet history is strewn with examples of drivers who have waited for what seems like an age to take that maiden triumph, only then to rattle off a whole succession of victories.

At Watkins Glen in 1969, Jochen Rindt scored his first Grand Prix win over five years after first racing a Formula One car. The following season he won again at Monaco, Zandvoort, Clermont-Ferrand, Silverstone and Hockenheim. Nigel Mansell was another who took five years to win for the first time, at Brands Hatch in the 1985 Grand Prix of Europe. He then won again in South Africa, the very next race. Similarly, Damon Hill took his first Grand Prix at

Hungary in 1993 – and went on to emerge victorious from the following two races as well.

Ron Dennis identified with Häkkinen's apparent dilemma. Always committed to playing to the strengths of not only his drivers, but all his employees, Dennis eventually took a unilateral decision to favour Häkkinen at Coulthard's expense at the 1997 European Grand Prix. There was no doubt in his mind that this was absolutely the correct course of action.

The race also presented a rare, almost unique opportunity. With Jacques Villeneuve and Michael Schumacher now head-to-head in a battle for the World Championship which involved neither of the McLaren drivers, Dennis pledged his team to keep out of the way of the title contestants. Ironically, he finished the day being forced to fend off allegations that he had collaborated with the Williams team deliberately to fix the result of this final round of the title chase.

Reports in the British press had suggested that Michael Schumacher, who faced a possible ban over his collision with Villeneuve, might rely on tapes of radio conversations between the Canadian driver and his pit as part of his defence when he appeared in front of an FIA World Council meeting in London. It was being speculated that these tapes had been recorded by the Ferrari team during the race and had been heard by Max Mosley, the FIA president, and F1 Commercial Rights Holder Bernie Ecclestone before being deliberately leaked to the media. Yet Dennis was quick to deny that McLaren had anything to feel ashamed of.

'Absolutely the opposite,' he insisted. 'The evidence of the race completely supports the fact that neither McLaren was ever in the way. The timing of these allegations could be seen by some as a smokescreen to deflect attention from the main issue facing Schumacher.

'On the Friday before the race at Jeréz, Villeneuve came to see me to apologize for the Japanese Grand Prix [the previous race on the Championship schedule] where he had slowed everybody down in the opening stages. At that race I had told Mika Häkkinen, our best-placed driver on the grid, that he had to be very careful not to get involved with either Villeneuve or Michael Schumacher, the two championship contestants.

'At Jeréz I reiterated to Frank Williams that there was no way our cars would get involved in the championship battle between the two contenders – and that if we were in the way, then we would get out of the way, even to the detriment of our own team's results.'

Dennis maintained that neither of his drivers was in any way disruptive. Coulthard, who had been running fourth behind Schumacher's Ferrari and ahead of Villeneuve after the Williams driver made his first refuelling stop, was called in early for his own first refuelling stop to get out of the Williams driver's way. The team did this despite the fact that Häkkinen's McLaren was due to stop first, as a result of which the Finnish driver lost time behind Heinz-Harald Frentzen's Williams and dropped behind Coulthard after his own first stop.

After the collision with Schumacher which eliminated the German driver's car from the race, Villeneuve's Williams was left lapping inconsistently in the lead, its driver grappling with serious tyre wear problems as a result of his car's suspension being knocked out of line when it smashed into the Ferrari.

'The two McLarens then caught up Giancarlo Fisichella's Jordan, which was a lap down but running between

Villeneuve and Coulthard who was now second,' continued Dennis. 'We then asked David to allow Häkkinen past from third place, which was only fair because he had lost more time early in the race.

'It took three laps for David to understand what we were asking and, although he was not amused when he finished the race, once the situation was fully explained, he totally accepted it. There is absolutely no truth that David was threatened with the sack if he did not move over.

'Then Fisichella moved out of the way and Häkkinen closed dramatically on Villeneuve who we thought was not going to resist our attack, which was quite logical because he only had to finish in the top six to clinch the championship. We knew he wasn't going to resist, so we went on the attack.'

Dennis took this opportunity to emphasize that all McLaren driver contracts contain clauses stating that no team orders will be given to drivers if they still have even an outside mathematical chance of winning the championship. 'It was the same when we had Niki Lauda, Alain Prost and Ayrton Senna driving for us throughout the history of our domination of the championship,' said Dennis. 'But on this occasion neither driver had any chance of the title, so we had the right to ask David to follow the team's instructions.'

No team instructions are given to a driver during the period in which he can *mathematically* win the World Championship. And mathematically means just that – no matter how unlikely it is in practice.

'But after that point has been reached, I think the team can justifiably expect that the drivers perform for the team before themselves. In our efforts not to interfere with the outcome of the World Championship, we reversed the first pit stop sequence previously agreed for Mika and David at Jeréz. David stopped first and that disadvantaged Mika, and therefore I decided when Villeneuve was clearly not going to resist any overtaking manoeuvre, to instruct David to reverse the order again.

'I don't have to justify that to anybody, and you might say it was a hollow win for Mika. But for him not to have won a race in his career, not through the lack of his own efforts, would not have been right. So I felt completely justified in taking off his shoulders for 1998 the psychological pressure of not having won a race.

'There were lots of races he should have won, but didn't. You might argue that this was a race he shouldn't have won, but he did. But I only reversed a situation which the team had already created and the disappointment which was clearly on David's face – and I'm being kind to myself saying disappointment – was due to the fact that there had been no dialogue before the race, and he couldn't understand why we were apparently being unfair to him.

'He felt understandably upset, feeling we were showing favouritism to Mika. But I hope, on reflection, David understood.'

What would Ron's reaction have been had Coulthard said, in effect, 'I hear what you're saying, but I just can't do it'? He smiles, slightly deflecting the question. 'The language over the radio between our team manager Dave Ryan and David was extremely colourful,' he admits.

'Perhaps I have even shaken David's faith in my or the team's even-handedness, but when I reflect on my years with McLaren, I feel comfortable that we have always acted with extreme fairness and balance to both drivers. I feel that, as time passes, David will understand that.

'He was not angry, not aggressive, but I clearly understand that there was that lingering doubt in his mind which can only be addressed with the passing of time.'

So, did Ron feel his two drivers liked each other? 'They don't dislike each other,' he replied. 'They are very different characters, both team players, both very committed and they both listen to people whose opinions they should listen to, but they have different lifestyles and backgrounds.

'So while they don't have the level of warmth you can sometimes see between team-mates, they do have a great deal of professional and mutual respect.

'Both of them carry with them, to different degrees, the frustration of not having the level of success they would like. That frustration manifests itself in different ways. It is the role of the management to be supportive and play to their strengths rather than their weaknesses. And that is what we do.'

Anybody present at the rostrum ceremony following that Jeréz race would have been able to read the body language of all three participants. Third-placed Jacques Villeneuve was naturally elated. He had won the World Championship in only his second season of F1 competition and his open, easy delight understandably washed over the tension which could be discerned between the two team-mates standing alongside him.

Coulthard, mentally reeling to come to terms with the hand he had been dealt, looked in a state of shock. His square-jawed profile was drawn taut, his lips pursed tightly together. As he wiped his face down with a towel, it would have been quite understandable and forgivable if he had shed the odd tear of abject frustration.

Even Häkkinen couldn't quite take it all in. The helter-skelter intensity of those last few laps had simply overwhelmed him. One minute he was third, the next hunting down Villeneuve to take the race lead on the final lap. In his own mind, he realized that he had driven better races than this, and he knew he would go on to score more impressive victories in the future. But for the moment, this would have to do. He had crossed his own personal Rubicon.

Of his relationship with his employer, he commented: 'Ron is a tough businessman, but a good friend. I don't want to say any more than that. At McLaren we work hard and play hard as a team.'

Yet Häkkinen keenly appreciated that the first win was a long time coming. Privately, during the summer of 1997 he was beginning to wonder if it ever would.

'I would fly to all the races throughout that season thinking to myself, "We're gonna win this one,"' he said. 'But, yes, there were times that I didn't think it would happen. And when I finally did win, I was surprised that perhaps I didn't feel quite so elated as I might have expected.

'Then I realized this was because, inwardly, I felt that I should have been winning Grands Prix as a matter of course for a long time. So it did not perhaps have quite the impact. It should have been normal.'

That said, Häkkinen confessed that if he hadn't scored that first victory at the end of 1997, he would have been under even greater strain at the start of 1998. 'It would have created more pressure,' he admits, 'but, as things transpired, winning in Melbourne was not a surprise. It just seemed natural.'

The boy was up and running.

# Chapter One

# Starting out

Mika Häkkinen was born on 28 September 1968. Six days earlier Denny Hulme had won the Canadian Grand Prix at Quebec's superb Mont Tremblant circuit. Driving a McLaren.

Eight days after the arrival of Harri and Aila Häkkinen's second child, Graham Hill won the United States Grand Prix at Watkins Glen. Driving a Lotus.

There is a certain poignancy here. At the time of writing this volume, Mika has driven only for those two teams in Formula One. He cut his Grand Prix teeth with Lotus, the famous British team that was treading the sunset road by the time he signed up for the 1990 season. And McLaren would carry him to sustained success in the sport's most senior category, including two World Championships.

The young lad enjoyed a comfortable, if not privileged upbringing. There was clearly much affection, laughter and zest for life in the Häkkinen family. It was an uncle who helped fire Mika's passion for karts, after which his parents supported him wholeheartedly.

The Häkkinens spent all their spare cash on supporting their son's racing efforts. They bought him his own off-the-peg Finkart in 1980, when Mika was eleven and a half. Quickly, he established himself as an outstanding talent in the rough-and-tumble of this pre-teenage crucible of burgeoning racing talent. Mika would grow up among a generation of Grand Prix drivers who had virtually all cut their teeth in this frantic wheel-to-wheel environment.

He won the Finnish Championships every year from 1983 to 1986. By this time Mika was firmly and irrevocably committed to circuit racing and, in his own mind, was set on one day becoming World Champion. Even during his teenage years, the young Häkkinen showed himself to be temperamentally self-contained and emotionally self-reliant.

As early as 1984 he crossed the path of a man who was to play a significant role in his future life as a formidably competitive rival. Travelling to the French Laval circuit, he found himself squaring up to a 14-year old German racer by the name of Michael Schumacher. Also contesting this event was the young American Paul Tracy, now one of the top Champcar drivers.

In 1987, Mika moved up into Formula Ford 1600, driving a Reynard which had previously been raced by his countryman J. J. Lehto, another protégé of Finland's former World Champion driver Keke Rosberg who had won the title back in '82 at the wheel of a Williams. This car took Häkkinen to triumph in the Finnish, Swedish and Nordic championships – quite enough to earn himself an invitation to a crucial test and evaluation session at the Donington Park circuit in Britain. This was staged by Philip Morris, whose long-term investment in all areas of international motorsport for more than a decade had established their Marlboro cigarette brand as motor racing's biggest single sponsor, probably of all time. Marlboro, a major sponsor of the McLaren team, always did more than its fair share when it came to nurturing fledgling talent.

In front of a judging panel which included McLaren boss Ron Dennis and former World Champion James Hunt, Häkkinen duly produced a competitive performance. The blond kid with the almost innocent expression may have seemed far removed from the macho image of a hard-nosed aspiring racer, but he clearly possessed one matchless attribute. He was ultimately quick and had the inner assurance to go with it.

In 1988 Häkkinen joined the young Scottish driver Allan McNish in the new Dragon Motorsports team contesting both the GM Vauxhall–Lotus Challenge in Britain and the Opel–Lotus Euroseries, several rounds of which took place on the support programme at European Grands Prix.

I'd briefly met McNish a year or so earlier and often took time off from the F1 paddock for a quick stroll down to the Opel–Lotus paddock to see how the new Scot was going. McNish, chatty and fluent, kept me vaguely in touch with this junior single-seater world, but Häkkinen was less communicative. He would smile broadly, but he came over as painfully shy and hesitant.

These were certainly not qualities reflected in his driving. At the end of a fraught 20-race season, he wound up second behind McNish in the British rankings, but won the European contest. In all, Häkkinen scored seven wins. It was sufficient to ensure that his Marlboro backing would be extended to fund his inevitable graduation into Formula 3 the following year.

After their closely matched season together in the hotly contested Vauxhall–Lotus category, the fortunes of Mika and Allan McNish diverged dramatically as they graduated on to the British Formula 3 Championship scene for 1989. Their experience with wings and slicks certainly stood them both in potentially good stead competitively; but the wrong choice of equipment has sunk many an ostensibly promising career, and so it proved for Häkkinen.

While McNish and the West Surrey Racing Ralt–Mugen frequently proved to be the class of the field, Häkkinen stayed with the Dragon squad to drive a Reynard–Toyota. Unfortunately, it proved to be far from the technical package guaranteed to allow a driver to do business at the sharp end of the F3 grids; but although Mika's pace was erratic as he struggled to gain top six placings, his pace was often sufficient to quicken heartbeats among spectators.

What worked particularly well for Mika was his ability to conjure heart-stoppingly quick laps out of nowhere, a talent which would one day prove one of his strongest single points as an F1 ace, There was no shortage of enthusiasm here, and his currency as a coming man survived the embarrassing reality that he had turned down the West Surrey team seat himself at the start of the year.

For all his ability, Mika could only manage seven top six finishes in this title battle, and an eventual distant seventh spot in the overall points table did little for his credibility. He was much better than that, all agreed. As if to underline what latent promise had been masked by these unfortunate circumstances, Häkkinen accepted a one-off drive in the West Surrey Ralt in the Cellnet SuperPrix at Brands Hatch in late October – and won in commanding fashion, seven seconds ahead of David Brabham.

This was precisely what the doctor ordered and Häkkinen, still benefiting from Marlboro's financial patronage, switched to the West Surrey operation for a second F3 season in 1990. There may have been a popular perception in British motor racing circles that if one failed to gain hard results during one's freshman F3 season there would be no second chance, but Häkkinen proved that this simply was not the case.

An added dash of tension was injected into the 1990 British F3 Championship by the acute rivalry between Häkkinen and his compatriot and namesake Mika Salo. They battled long and hard with their Ralt–Mugen Hondas prepared respectively by West Surrey and Alan Docking Racing. There was a sharp edge to the competition between the two men which, during the course of a frenzied season, boiled over into a couple of instances of too-close contact.

During the month of June a particularly robust confrontation between the Finns at Silverstone, where the two Mikas collided heavily, left Häkkinen sidelined from the race and their mutual relationship about as frosty and strained as it could get.

Another key episode followed in August, at the point where Salo stood poised effectively to wipe out Häkkinen's F3 Championship aspirations. He was leading easily with three laps to go – only to spin over the gravel trap at Russell Corner at Snetterton, an unforced error which allowed Häkkinen through to win.

That victory was the first of five for the future McLaren–Mercedes driver, a series which would enable him to clinch the F3 crown with two races still to go. Much of the credit for this transformation must be given to Dick Bennetts, the team owner who had presided over Ayrton Senna's talent during his electrifying 1993 British F3 campaign.

Häkkinen's qualifying performance in 1990 was simply extraordinary, amounting to 11 pole positions as compared with Salo's four. Bennetts' contribution was to help Häkkinen further refine that remarkable skill, while at the same time tutoring him in the subtleties of racemanship.

Meanwhile, the management of Häkkinen's racing and business career was being steered by Keke Rosberg. At the time of writing the 50-year old millionaire has been steering Häkkinen's career effectively and unobtrusively for a decade. Well seasoned in the unpredictable ways of the motor racing business, at one and the same time he displays an almost paternal interest in the progress of his protégé while never obviously impinging on either his personality or his progress.

In a country with a modest population of five million and a long established reputation for producing world-class rally drivers, Rosberg was Finland's first World Champion racing driver. He achieved that distinction at the wheel of a non-turbo-charged Williams FW08 at the start of the Formula One turbo-charged engine era, and battled manfully against more powerful opposition to clinch his title.

During his racing career, Rosberg gained a reputation for a cocky cheerfulness which stopped just short of obvious arrogance. Having lived away from Finland since he was just out his teens, Keke quickly gained a cosmopolitan gloss lacking in many of his compatriots. From an early stage in his career he made sure he was paid for driving racing cars, and became very adept at striking a good bargain.

After he retired from the McLaren F1 team at the end of 1986, Keke sat down and realized that he was as well qualified as any of the breed of so-called 'professional managers' to help the careers of young drivers. Better, in fact, because he could harness his first-hand expertise to deal with such a new challenge.

So how did he start out in the driver management game? 'I was in a hotel room in Helsinki back in 1987 a month or two after I'd driven my last Grand Prix,' he recalled.

'I was talking to J. J. Lehto, who was then a 20-year old Finnish Formula Ford racer. I was always planning to get involved in management, but had believed that I would need a year or so to get my thoughts sorted out once I had retired.

'So here is this blond lad in front of me and my first conversation with him was enough to convince me that it was now or never as far as driver management was concerned. I had one goal before I retired. I thought that when I stopped I would try for the unbelievable and try to make another Finnish F1 driver.'

He concedes that the fact that he is a former driver gives him an advantage, if not a decisive one. 'I would like to think that the real advantage is that people know me, they know I'm a hard worker, an honest person trying to do the best for my drivers. And I think my drivers feel the same about me too. I put a high price on having a good reputation.'

Those who work closely with Rosberg confirm that he displays qualities very similar to those which were evident when he was racing. He works hard, knows when to push and has a keen knowledge of commercial etiquette. In short, he demonstrates business savvy.

In the early days it was very much a hands-on business.

'One day I was organizing a work permit, the next grooming their appearance for some official engagement or other,' he said. 'Getting them – Häkkinen and Lehto – organized with everything. Arranging residency for them in Monte Carlo because I'd said from the beginning that I would manage the business from Monaco and so, mostly for practical reasons, needed them there. Phone sex is not the same as the real thing!

'So it works better for them and, having managed to build happy surroundings for myself in Monte Carlo, it worked very well for me too.'

Over the years Keke and his management company have looked after Häkkinen well. In 1990, when the younger Finn was poised on the verge of winning the British Formula 3 championship, he was stopped at Heathrow Airport by an over-zealous customs official who believed that foreign racing drivers required work permits.

'He was deported back to Helsinki only days before the final race of the year,' said Rosberg, 'but fortunately Mrs Thatcher was just about to make an official visit to Finland and the matter was very quickly sorted out with the British embassy.'

A year later, Rosberg negotiated a deal which saw Häkkinen moving up into Formula One. The new Lotus team manager, Peter Collins, had held a similar post at Williams during Keke's time there and the two men got on well.

A partnership between Rosberg's driver and his former Williams collaborator seemed the next logical move. And so it proved.

# Chapter Two

# Into Formula One

Mika Häkkinen graduated into Formula One at the start of the 1991 season driving for one of the most famous names in the Grand Prix firmament: Lotus. Yet despite all the prestige surrounding the team originally founded by Colin Chapman almost 40 years previously, the lustrous gloss of a World Championship winning organization was but a faded memory.

Chapman had died, prematurely and unexpectedly, from a sudden heart attack in December 1982, since when his beloved racing team had been locked into a persistent decline. Initially the dip in performance was barely perceptible, buttressed as it was by the driving genius of Ayrton Senna during the years 1985–7. But once Senna quit the team for McLaren, the downward slope steepened dramatically into a nosedive to apparent oblivion.

At the end of the 1988 season Lotus lost its Honda engine supply contract. This meant that for 1989 engines had to be paid for out of a Camel cigarette sponsorship budget, around 50 per cent of which was already committed to Nelson Piquet's reputed $3 million dollar retainer. Times were hard, and were set to get even harder, notwithstanding additional sponsorship from Japanese sources which supported Satoru Nakajima's presence in the second car.

The Chapman family had one final serious F1 push in 1990 under the technical direction of the highly respected Tony Rudd. A deal was forged for the team to use Lamborghini V12 engines and a completely new driver squad, Derek Warwick and Martin Donnelly, was recruited. But nothing much changed; and an already pretty dismal season was made considerably worse when Donnelly crashed heavily while practising for the Spanish Grand Prix at Jeréz. He was lucky to escape with his life from an accident which ended his professional racing career.

Although the Chapmans now decided to call time on the official Lotus F1 operation, they were certainly not averse to its continuation in approved private hands. Thus, with the Chapmans' blessing, the use of the team and its operational assets were effectively leased to a triumvirate consisting of Peter Collins, Peter Wright and German F3 team owner Horst Schubel.

Collins was an ambitious former Lotus employee who had worked for the team as long ago as 1979 on his arrival from Australia. Born in Sydney, Collins had been brought up only a short distance from the Warwick Farm circuit which hosted many rounds of the prestigious Tasman Championship during his teenage years in the mid-1960s.

'My interest had been sparked off by my brother, who was acting as a mechanic to a friend's racing team,' he recalled, 'and it didn't take me long to realize that I wanted to become part of the scene. Not as a mechanic, because I didn't have the right sort of qualifications, but something perhaps on the administrative side.'

After trying his hand in the travel business and jour-nalism, he also acted as a part-time press liaison officer for

Warwick Farm, which was being run by the expatriate Englishman Geoff Sykes. Collins was quick to admit that Sykes helped him enormously when it came to developing a lot of contacts within the British motor racing industry.

Collins finally made a breakthrough in 1978 when he began a long series of interviews with Lotus, eventually joining the famous Norfolk-based squad as assistant team manager the following year. Ultimately he rose to the status of team manager, although he reflected that 'they didn't seem to like official titles there.'

At the start of 1982 he spent a short spell managing the ATS team before being invited by Frank Williams to join his team, which boasted Keke Rosberg as the number one driver, as racing manager. He had held this position for three years when in 1985 he was approached by Benetton.

'Rory Byrne was asked to talk to me at Monaco that year,' he recalled. 'At that stage Benetton only had a minor shareholding in the team, but it was pretty clear which way things were going. This was very important to me because I needed to be sure that the team's future was secure and properly financed before making such an important career decision. But I was convinced.'

Collins moved over to the Benetton team and remained there for the next four seasons. Yet this sort of responsibility could only take him so far. Running his own show was the overwhelming priority; and, having introduced British rising star Johnny Herbert into the team in 1989, Collins left later that year and laid plans to go it alone. Hence the arrangement with Lotus; and, once he'd struck the deal with his old employer, it seemed that he was on his way.

But these were nerve-wracking times. Collins had been working on the programme since the summer of 1989 when he had been appointed as a marketing consultant with a brief to find sufficient funds to ensure that Team Lotus would continue.

'Things were getting pretty tight by the end of November [1990],' recalls the man who originally left Australia together with his wife Jane and just £150 between them in January 1978.'But we managed to get a package of funds together which would keep the company open through December and into January 1991. That gave us time to put other things in place and come out with the positive press statement that Lotus was continuing, and that we would be using Judd V8 engines.'

Over that crucial winter, not a penny more than was necessary was spent by the team. Circumstances dictated the use of the old 102 moulds to produce a sturdy chassis for the Judd EV V9. Drawings for the planned Lotus 103 had to be scrapped. The new project was insufficiently far advanced and, in any event, Collins knew that any new car simply had to pass the mandatory FISA crash test in early February 1991. If it failed, and needed revamping, then Team Lotus would not make it to the first race.

Under the new management consortium, Lotus would be fielding interim Lotus-type 102B chassis derived from the previous year's Lamborghini-engined machines. However, motive power would now be provided by the Judd EV V8 engines which were available on lease arrangements from the British preparation specialist.

During his time at Williams, Collins had developed a very positive relationship with Rosberg. He admired the Finn's no-nonsense approach to his chosen profession and thoroughly approved of Keke's habit of calling a spade a spade. You always knew where you were with Rosberg.

The team was desperately keen to raise as much finance as possible, and Rosberg was equally keen to get his young protégé Mika Häkkinen into F1 at the first realistic opportunity. Having won the 1990 British Formula 3 Championship, Mika was clearly ready for the big break.

The opening round of the 1991 World Championship took place on the makeshift circuit through the streets of Phoenix, Arizona. Team Lotus arrrived there intent on taking the first step towards restoring their tattered reputation under the new management structure. They were short on finance and resources, but nevertheless projected a brisk and businesslike image with just enough British racing green livery on their cars to quicken the hearts of those fans who could remember the days when the name 'Lotus' was uttered with the same reverence now accorded to 'McLaren'.

Häkkinen quickly got to grips with the business of F1, despite minimal pre-race testing. The 22-year-old qualified his Lotus 102B 13th on the grid, lapping more than two seconds faster than his team-mate, the British driver Julian Bailey, who had enterprisingly raised his own finance to buy the drive and had been nominally recruited as a paying stand-in until Martin Donnelly was ready to return. Bailey failed to make the cut after suffering engine trouble during the second qualifying session and being forced to squeeze into the hastily adapted cockpit of Mika's car after the Finn had finished with it on Saturday afternoon. It proved a vain effort.

Even at this early stage of the year it was clear that Häkkinen had staked his claim on the number one seat; but his F1 debut was destined to be a fraught affair by any standards.

Early on in the race, as Mika had accelerated hard over one particularly violent bump on this challenging street circuit, one of his knees bounced up and tripped the quick-release collar retaining the removable steering wheel. Suddenly, he realized he was losing steering input. He dived for the pit lane to check the wheel, and then made a second stop to replace it. The problem solved, Mika resumed to pound along stoically at the back of the pack until an oil union worked loose and he was forced to retire with an engine bay oil fire.

'Mika was blindingly quick, right from the word go in Phoenix,' said Peter Wright in 1999. 'The fact that he was a bit on the long and gangling side was responsible for the fact that his knee tripped the steering wheel securing collar.

'He was a typical Finn, I suppose you could say. He lacked maturity at that early stage and didn't really have much in the way of technical input. He could tell you what the car was doing, but not really why it was doing it. He only had a very basic grasp of English, of course, and was prone to having mid-race slumps when he slowed his pace slightly and then picked up speed again. It might have been because he needed to be a little fitter, I'm not certain.'

Häkkinen had done well enough on his F1 debut, but he urgently needed to develop a psychological veneer of resilience. The kid was going to have a difficult season and would struggle to sustain anything approaching a mid-grid position.

The lack of a spare car frustrated Lotus's efforts when it came to the Brazilian Grand Prix on São Paulo's rutted and ill-kempt Interlagos circuit. Just as in Phoenix, Bailey found himself having to share Häkkinen's Lotus 102B after his own encountered technical problems. Again the Englishman failed to make the cut while Häkkinen got on to the grid in 22nd place.

Come the race, he kept running steadily to finish in eighth place, albeit three laps behind Ayrton Senna's winning McLaren–Honda. Two and a half years later he would be Ayrton's team-mate and set fair for stardom.

The third round of the 1991 title chase was the San Marino Grand Prix at Imola, a race which left a bitter-sweet taste in the mouth of the Team Lotus personnel. Saturday morning brought with it the dreadful news that David Jacques, one of the team's mechanics, had died in hospital, having been unconscious ever since falling through a skylight at the local hotel while at Imola for pre-race tests the previous weekend. Both Häkkinen and Bailey wore black armbands out of respect for the remainder of the weekend.

Under the circumstances, good runs to fifth and sixth places were seen as worthwhile rewards for the small British team, Häkkinen and Bailey respectively gaining the first points of their F1 Championship careers.

Perhaps unsurprisingly, this was as far as it went for Häkkinen and Lotus in 1991. The two points they scored together at Imola remained their sole foray into the top six finishers. Yet Häkkinen did well enough in other races, posting ninth place in Mexico City and 12th at Silverstone, both fast circuits. Taking into account that he was giving away around 90 bhp to the fastest cars in the field, he was doing well. Lotus reckoned they had discovered something of a hidden jewel. But it wasn't to last.

Throughout 1991, Team Lotus had been very much a no-frills operation. There were no fees for the drivers, no business-class air tickets for the management. They squeezed by on around £7 million, small change by the standards of F1's front-runners. For the whole of what Collins was wont to describe as 'a holding season', Lotus was borrowing heavily to invest for the future. It purchased the old Williams wind tunnel, signed Chris Murphy from Leyton House to head the design team, and finally, against the apparent odds, clinched a deal to run Cosworth–Ford HB V8 engines for the 1992 World Championship campaign.

Unfortunately, for the 1992 season Rosberg lost Häkkinen's Marlboro sponsorship. It could have been a hammer blow to the young Finn's chances, but Peter Collins was absolutely convinced of his talent. He agreed that Mika should stay on the payroll.

In the second season of its resurgence under the stewardship of the Peters Collins and Wright, Lotus ditched its leased Judd V8s and opted instead for the more costly 75-degree Ford HB customer engine which was leased from Cosworth. With around 730 bhp at 13,500 rpm on tap, it meant that Häkkinen and his team-mate Johnny Herbert went into battle with around 40 bhp less than the pace-setting Williams–Renaults handled by Nigel Mansell and Riccardo Patrese.

Lotus had heady ambitions which, with the matchless benefit of hindsight, would lead them to becoming financially over-committed. Bearing in mind the upbeat optimism with which the team faced the 1992 season, it was difficult to believe that they only had three seasons separating them from effective bankruptcy.

For the moment, however, the mood was positive and ambitious. Peter Wright, who had masterminded the Lotus team's active suspension development for much of the 1980s, was keen to develop this further in the interests of enhanced competitiveness.

Although the new Lotus 107 designed by Chris Murphy was fitted with conventional 'passive' suspension on its race debut at Imola – the team had started the year with an uprated 1991 chassis – it was decided early on in the programme to incorporate a very straightforward and light mechanical/hydraulic-controlled 'reactive' suspension system. With the basic suspension utilizing conventional spring/dampers, the 107 could be raced in reactive or passive form, the transition being made simply by de-activating the control computer. The engineering team concentrating on this aspect of the car's performance was further strengthened by the arrival of John Miles – whose brief was to concentrate solely on suspension development – shortly before the first race of the season at Kyalami.

The famous South African circuit near Johannesburg was playing host to F1 for the first time since 1985. Sadly for many racing insiders, the newly developed track was a far cry from the heart-wrenchingly dramatic old Kyalami. Not the same at all, in fact, as the venue where we could remember spectators almost physically leaping back from the fence as Keke Rosberg had slammed through the old Jukskei kink, a climbing, flat-out left-hander which he took, without feathering the throttle, at around 150 mph with 1,000 bhp on tap from his Williams–Honda during qualifying when F1 cars last visited the area.

Häkkinen's first experience of the circuit was hardly encouraging. It was Herbert's turn to have a trouble-free run to 11th on the grid; for Mika, all the cards fell against him. Things started going wrong on Friday when his car was beset first by an oil leak and then in the afternoon by a clutch problem, forcing him to take the spare car which had been set up for Herbert. On Saturday he over-revved his Ford HB engine during the morning and again had to take the spare car for the afternoon. He ended up 21st, dejected and disappointed. There was a particular problem here which needed to be addressed.

Mika found himself having difficulties with his gear-change technique early in the year. Mating the old Lamborghini-based gearbox on the 102D with the particular characteristics of the Ford HB engine was a persistent problem, and he never felt quite happy with this set-up. Eventually he would be coaxed into modifying his technique. Lotus could ill afford $100,000 rebuild fees caused by straightforward over-revving.

That first race of the 1992 season went pretty well for Lotus, all things considered. As Mansell and Patrese headed for a convincing success in first and second places, Herbert made it home in sixth to score a Championship point, and Mika nipped ahead of Michele Alboreto's Footwork on the very last lap to take ninth overall. Considering how far back on the grid he had started, this was certainly a consistent and respectable performance.

The second round of the '92 title chase was the Mexican Grand Prix at the bumpy, rutted Autodromo Hermanos Rodriguez. Mika was 11th fastest at the end of the first day – a fine effort on this extremely demanding circuit where a power deficit tended to show up dramatically – but he rather blotted his copybook the following day when, once again, he missed a gear shift and damaged the engine. Again it meant a switch to the spare car – and a flicker of a frown from Peter Collins – followed by a gradual slide down to 18th in the final starting order. Not a good omen.

Come the race, however, Mika produced a simply epic performance. Gradually climbing through the pack in a race punctuated by many technical problems among the opposition, he pulled through to seventh place with 32 of the 69 laps completed.

Immediately ahead of the Finn's Lotus ran Jean Alesi's Ferrari, but a light blue haze emanating from the rear of the Italian car told its own story. The Ferrari's engine was about to expire terminally, as Häkkinen had become only too well aware. So much oil was pouring out over his helmet visor that he quickly ran out of 'tear-offs' and had to race on with his visor raised, crouching low in the cockpit to minimize the discomfort such a technique inevitably involved.

At the end of the afternoon Mika was rewarded with a fine sixth place ahead of Herbert, both the Lotus drivers having done a very good job of embarrassing their more experienced and better-funded opposition for much of the weekend.

Grand Prix racing has a habit of dishing up painful frustrations to its competitors. Just when you think you are making steady progress in the right direction, the whole house can come down on your head with little in the way of warning. So it was for Lotus at Interlagos for the third round of the '92 title contest.

The bumpy and dusty São Paulo track left both Lotus 102Ds struggling dramatically for grip. As a result, on this occasion both drivers came painfully close to not qualifying.

In the end they made the cut only in 24th and 26th place, Mika just pipping Johnny by a scant 0.1 seconds. The race itself was best forgotten. Mika finished four laps behind Mansell's winning Williams, tenth and last, while Herbert retired following a collision not of his making.

Lack of grip was also a problem at Barcelona's Circuit de Catalunya, where the Spanish Grand Prix took place as the fourth round of the World Championship. Häkkinen and Herbert qualified 21st and 26th respectively, Mika at least getting a slight leg-up from a change of chassis set-up late in the qualifying session. Compounding Lotus's disappointment, the race took place in conditions of torrential rain and both drivers spun off into retirement on the treacherous track surface.

Herbert gave the new Lotus 107 its debut in the San Marino Grand Prix at Imola but retired early with gearbox problems. Still, at least the Englishman made the start. Häkkinen was bedevilled by gearbox and fuel feed problems which prevented him from getting into the swing of things, as a result of which he failed to make the cut for the first time in his brief F1 career.

For the traditional scramble through the streets of Monaco, Lotus arrived still with only a single 107 on hand for Johnny Herbert which the Englishman managed to muscle on to the grid in an amazing ninth place. For his part, Häkkinen spent the first day struggling with the elderly 102D. The second 107 was completed at the team's base in Norfolk only just in time to be freighted down to the Principality for Saturday's second qualifying session.

By this stage of the game Lotus was worryingly short of spare parts for the new car: not a particularly reassuring state of affairs to contemplate at Monaco, where the risk of removing a suspension component against unyielding concrete walls is an ever-present worry.

Mika was told 'not to risk anything', a warning which hardly helped focus his mind, and he also found himself uncomfortable with the fit of the cockpit of the new car. Despite this, and with his legs knocking against the underside of the steering rack, he battled with an inoperative clutch to qualify 14th. By any standards, it was a truly great performance.

In the race, Mika climbed to ninth place before the clutch broke for good and Herbert crashed. Lotus now held joint sixth place in the Constructors' Championship points table, equalled by Footwork and Tyrrell. They were starting to make heavy weather against an increasingly difficult tide.

As the summer of 1992 unfolded, Lotus was coming to terms with an uncomfortable truth, something so fundamental to the business of F1 that nobody even bothers to think about it; it is simply taken it for granted. The fact is that attempting to make up ground by honing and developing a new technical development, something one hopes will offer a performance advantage in the future, risks undermining the fortnightly pressure to achieve hard results with the existing equipment at one's disposal.

So it was for Häkkinen at Lotus. He retired with gearbox failure in Canada, but then at Magny-Cours for the French Grand Prix it seemed as though the spiral had been reversed when he did an excellent job to qualify 11th, reverting to the passive suspension set-up after experiencing problems with the reactive system during qualifying.

In the race Häkkinen and Herbert finished fourth and fifth, vaulting Lotus into fifth place in the Constructors' points table. Their position was strengthened by Häkkinen's sixth place in the British Grand Prix at Silverstone a week later, although the spectre of another gearbox problem cast its shadow across Johnny Herbert's bold effort and he failed to make it to the chequered flag.

Lotus then paid the price of missing the test session prior to the German Grand Prix at Hockenheim, both Herbert and Häkkinen complaining that their 107s felt over-sensitive and extremely nervous to drive. They nevertheless qualified a promising 11th and 13th, with Herbert just ahead of his team-mate on this occasion, but engine problems meant that neither Lotus driver made it to the finishing line.

In the Hungarian Grand Prix, Häkkinen did a superb job to finish fourth on a day which saw Herbert spinning off on the opening lap trying to avoid a collision between Erik Comas and Thierry Boutsen. Throughout the gruelling 77-lap event, Mika drove with great verve and determination, getting ahead of Martin Brundle's Benetton with four laps to go and looking as though he might even catch Gerhard Berger's McLaren–Honda for third place.

Unfortunately, his final lap proved unexpectedly dramatic. Half a dozen corners from home his engine died momentarily as he changed down to fourth and the car went into an unexpected spin. For a fleeting moment it seemed as though Brundle would retake the position, but the Englishman had to run wide to avoid the gyrating Lotus, which allowed Häkkinen sufficient time to squeeze back on the circuit, keep his position and finish fourth after all.

The Belgian Grand Prix saw Mika garner another point for a sixth place finish in a race punctuated by heavy rain showers. The same race saw Michael Schumacher's first win for Benetton. If you had said that it would be another five years before Häkkinen celebrated a similarly historic moment in his own personal career, you would have been laughed out of the F1 paddock at Spa. Yet there was still a very long way to go.

Ten days later came a crucial event which, indirectly, would put the Finn on the road to fame and fortune. In the run-up to the Italian Grand Prix, McLaren convened a press conference in New York where it was announced that Champcar star Michael Andretti would be joining the team as Ayrton Senna's team-mate for the 1993 season.

Ron Dennis explained that one of the key reasons behind signing Andretti was his ability to overtake. 'That may seem obvious,' said the McLaren boss, 'but I think that Michael is probably in that small band of perhaps five drivers in the world who have the necessary aggression in traffic and the desire to win.' In the event, the decision to sign Andretti turned out to be one of the rare occasions on which Dennis's racing savvy let him down.

Meanwhile, Häkkinen continued through to the end of the season at the wheel of his Lotus, bagging another two points for fifth place in the Portuguese Grand Prix By the end of the 1992 season, Häkkinen's face had lost its youthful, almost chubby bloom. The boy was turning into a man. Lotus ended up a very respectable fifth in the Constructors' Championship on 13 points; and the lion's share of these had been racked up by the blond Finn.

Moreover, Häkkinen continued to benefit from Rosberg's tutelage, and his performances became increasingly reminiscent of the style demonstrated by the senior Finn in his F1 heyday, a heady blend of epic car control and increasingly extrovert insouciance.

# Chapter Three

# The fork in the road

In 1992 Keke Rosberg had found himself having to put his hand in his own pocket to keep alive his young driver's dreams of championship glory.

'Marlboro withdrew their financial support for Mika at the end of January 1992,' he said, 'and this proved impossible to replace. I ended up paying for Mika to stay at Lotus that year, but it wasn't a question of saying "Does it make sense to put money in there or not?" because I'd always said that I would never invest my own money in motor racing.

'But since this was really my problem – in the sense that it was really my failure to have got the necessary funds together – I had to put the money in. If I hadn't taken that decision then Mika's career would have been over. So there really was no choice.'

It was clear that something would have to be negotiated afresh for the 1993 season. By the end of the summer of '92 Mika's profile and image were growing apace. He reminded many onlookers of the legendary Swedish driver Ronnie Peterson who'd been one of the very quickest F1 exponents of the 1970s. He had the same aura of Nordic calm, the blond hair and the apparently impassive demeanour. Like Ronnie, he also seemed to be programmed to drive flat out. Nothing less.

By the late summer it was clear that the dominant Williams–Renault squad might have a vacancy. Nigel Mansell, who had clinched his World Championship title with second place in the Hungarian Grand Prix in mid-August, was now playing hardball over the terms of a new contract for 1993. But Renault also wanted Frank to take Alain Prost as team leader, the French triple champion having sat out the '92 season after an acrimonious breach with Ferrari the previous autumn.

Perhaps inevitably, the Williams/Mansell negotiations fell apart, prompting speculation that Ayrton Senna might switch from McLaren. On the rostrum at Monza, having won the 1992 Italian Grand Prix, Ayrton had remarked enigmatically to second-placed Martin Brundle: 'So it's you and me next year at Williams, then.' Brundle was slightly taken aback by this, but it obviously wasn't going to happen. With Prost joining the Williams–Renault squad there was no way in for Senna, Alain being unwilling to experience a renewal of the friction they had experienced as partners in the McLaren–Honda squad in 1988/9.

Rosberg also began talking to Frank Williams; and it may be that Frank Williams sometimes sits and reflects on just what a talent he let slip away when he changed his mind about signing up Mika Häkkinen.

It was towards the end of 1992, when the Finn had been racing for two years with Lotus, when Keke began negotiating with Frank for him to drive with Alain Prost the following year. The two men thought they were close to a deal. Then Frank unaccountably changed his mind. Rosberg, who as a former Williams driver knew what made the team boss tick, was shrewd enough not to press the point. 'If he was uncomfortable with the deal, then it wouldn't have worked,' he later reflected.

The next crucial fork in the road for Häkkinen's career came at the end of that same season when McLaren Managing Director Ron Dennis offered him a testing contract for 1993. There was another option on the table, a race contract with Ligier, but that did not seem to offer the same long-term potential.

Rosberg, who had driven for Dennis in Formula Two during the 1970s and later partnered Alain Prost in the 1986 McLaren line-up, knew that he was negotiating with a friend as regards Häkkinen's future. But it was still a difficult call.

'I had known Ron for many years, but it is always difficult to assess how much such a friendship counts for when you start to do business,' said Rosberg. 'But when Ron said, "Yes, we're going to do a deal with you," I knew I hadn't got to worry. Our friendship was such that I knew his word was enough to count on. 'So I rang Ron and asked, "Are you ready to move now on Mika?" It's two days before Christmas and Ron's skiing at Courcheval while Mika is on a plane down from Helsinki, although he doesn't know why.'

Rosberg and Häkkinen stayed up until the small hours debating whether Mika should go to Ligier to race or sign up to the testing contract with McLaren.

'Mika and I talked all night and he was convinced that going to McLaren as test driver was the right thing,' recalled Keke. 'When I was doing this Mika deal I was more worried about it than at any time in my own racing career. My ambition and determination to do the best job just didn't let me sleep. If I see the possibility of failure, however remote, then I feel an incredible burden of responsibility.'

Yet the passage of time gives a welcome and overdue perspective to the frantic intensity of the moment. When Rosberg was juggling the deals for Häkkinen at the end of the 1992 season, the future was hardly clear-cut and unambiguous. There was no black and white in terms of how Mika's career path might unfold.

There was also the underlying sense of bewilderment over Frank Williams's attitude. What was he thinking about? Häkkinen was clearly one of the most impressive young rising stars in the F1 business, so why did he approach Rosberg with the offer of a contract if he did not really want to pursue that option? Whatever his reasoning, in the end he opted for Damon Hill's services.

Keke was sufficiently seasoned in the way of the Williams team to realize that it would be imprudent to push the issue too hard. 'But I was amazed,' he later confided.

'It wasn't the amazement of Frank Williams apparently being uncomfortable with the prospect of the deal, it was amazement that after I'd worked my butt off I was told simply, "We're not going to do this." 'Immediately the Williams case turned sour, we started negotiating with Ligier.'

This in itself was something of an ironic coincidence, for Damon Hill was also talking to Ligier about a possible drive for 1993. The French team, he judged, could usefully tap into his experience with the Renault V10 engine which both Williams and Ligier were using.

Privately, of course, Damon was hoping that his established role as Williams test driver would be enough to secure his promotion to the race team once Nigel Mansell headed off to the USA for his CART odyssey. And Damon's judgement in this was pretty sound.

None of this exactly delighted Peter Collins. He felt that Lotus had been ill-rewarded for the groundwork they had carried out in helping Häkkinen to establish his F1 credentials. But, although Lotus believed it had an ongoing deal with Mika, the FIA Contract Recognition Board ruled that it did not have a binding contract. Häkkinen was free to move to McLaren at precisely the moment that his increasing status would have been an asset for Lotus in the uphill quest for sponsorship. Yet that is the uncompromising – cruel, if you like – nature of F1. It is a case of survival of the fittest, with the smaller, underfinanced teams historically fulfilling the role of training grounds for the prestige, front-line operations. Collins put on as brave a face as possible and knuckled down to tackle the future.

For his part, the McLaren team chief Ron Dennis was hedging his bets – carefully, and with meticulous precision. After a disappointing 1992 season, Ayrton Senna had left Europe to winter as usual at his beach house in Brazil. He was extremely annoyed with the fact that Honda had withdrawn from F1 at the end of the season, thereby depriving McLaren of a works engine deal, and had also been frustrated over the manner in which the Japanese company had fallen away in terms of commitment to technical development in the second half of the season.

And, although he would be the last to admit it, Ayrton was also brooding over the fact that he'd been kept out of Williams by Prost's apparent intransigence. In many ways a deep and sensitive personality, Senna was notably unsentimental when it came to his motor racing prospects. If the best car was provided by another team, then he obviously hankered for a place in that team. Not that Senna needed to make any approaches, of course. Most F1 team owners would have crawled six miles over shards of broken glass to meet him if they thought there was a chance of a deal. Ayrton knew that, which made his annoyance over Prost's attitude all the more intense.

Meanwhile, back in Britain, Dennis played his hand as cautiously as he dared. Ironically, just as Rosberg was talking with Ligier about a possible seat for Mika, so Ron was talking to them as well. He wanted to buy the team as a means of accessing their Renault V10 engine contract. The deal was that the Renaults would then be switched to McLaren and Ron would engineer another source of engine supply for the French team.

Renault gave its blessing to the proposal, and the plan was that the McLaren–Renaults would run on Shell fuel and lubricants for their first season. But then Elf, Renault's long-time fuel and oil partner, put a spoke in the wheel by vetoing the use of Shell products. Dennis was not willing to breach his existing commitment to Shell; so the deal fell through.

There is no doubt that the prospect of a McLaren–Renault would have set Senna's eyes blazing with anticipation. But it was not to be. Instead, McLaren was going to have to pay for its engines. It entered a partnership with British engine specialists Cosworth for supplies of its compact Ford HB V8 engine, an investment which involved the team in an outlay of £6 million in lease fees.

There were all manner of complicating elements to the McLaren–Ford equation and, as it turned out, most of them would have indirect knock-on consequences which were distinctly in Mika Häkkinen's favour.

The very first problem came in the autumn of 1992. It was McLaren's customary practice to start designing their new F1 cars in the September prior to the season in which they were scheduled to race. But this time it was different. Delays in finalizing precisely which engine would be used resulted in the deal with Cosworth not being sewn up until December. Although McLaren's state-of-the-art computer-aided design system enabled much of this lost ground to be made up, the fact remained that the new MP4/8-Cosworth Ford V8 was not ready to test until early February, barely a month before the first race at Kyalami.

This mattered not one iota to Senna. From the moment he hopped into its cockpit at Silverstone three weeks before the first race, he was right on the pace. But Michael Andretti was desperately short of miles in which to acclimatize himself to the business of F1 racing. Sure, Honda's engine supply deal had lasted to the end of the year, enabling him to get some miles under his belt in the old MP4/7A; but in the New Year there followed a frustrating six-week gap without any running.

Dennis also had problems on another front. As far as the public were concerned, Senna was only committing himself to the team on a race-by-race basis. And he was demanding £625,000 per race as his fee. This was quite a tab even for McLaren to pick up, but Ron agreed. And yet he took Mika down to Kyalami for the first race of the season, perhaps not quite certain whether or not the Brazilian would actually turn up.

From the start of the year, Ron promised that Mika 'would get a race sometime this season'. It seemed a distinctly enigmatic observation. Was he anticipating Michael Andretti's failure to make the grade?

Probably not. More likely, he was contemplating the awful prospect of Senna sitting out a couple of races because he wasn't satisfied with the situation he was in, either the financial deal or the fact that the McLaren MP4/8 wasn't quick enough to seriously mix it with the Williams–Renaults.

From the start of the season, Häkkinen just got on with his allotted test work, quietly and unobtrusively integrating himself within the McLaren squad. The young Finn rapidly impressed all who worked with him. He was pleasant, willing to learn at every opportunity – and clearly quick enough to get the job done.

Meanwhile, Andretti was struggling. He started the season on a bad note with crashes at Kyalami and Interlagos, then spun off at Donington Park on the opening lap in torrential rain, conditions that provided the backdrop for possibly Senna's most brilliant win. From then on Michael scored points on only three occasions. The last of these, ironically, was Monza, where he finished third, gaining his sole F1 podium placing – after the decision had been taken to dispense with his services for the rest of the year.

Step forward Mika Häkkinen, your moment has arrived.

Mika took over the second McLaren MP4/8 in time for the Portuguese Grand Prix at Estoril, where he really rattled Senna's cage by outqualifying the Brazilian for third place. By any standards this was a tremendous performance, and the smile of sheer pleasure which radiated across his face was a pleasant contrast indeed to the glum countenances so often seen elsewhere in the F1 pit lane.

'I think I could have done even better,' said Mika. 'I really don't mind this format of having a limited number of laps in practice [a new rule for 1993] because it puts more pressure on me and I go better as a result. But I haven't yet fully got back into the discipline of the business and I think I could have produced a little more, perhaps.'

For his part, Senna had no complaints about his car to excuse his own performance and he was the first to congratulate his young team-mate on his achievement. As another McLaren team member commented: 'I haven't seen Senna being made to work as hard as that since Alain Prost was here. Anyway, it's nice to be back to running a proper two-car team.'

Not that Prost would be particularly impressed with Mika's driving when it came to the run to the first corner at the start of the race. With pole qualifier Damon Hill being forced to start at the back of the grid after a starting mechanism problem had caused his Williams FW15C to stall just prior to the final parade lap, Häkkinen had a clear track ahead of him and the chance to run round the outside of Prost's Williams, which was the other front-row qualifier.

Häkkinen squeezed the Frenchman relentlessly and Alain did not mince his words later. 'If I did one-tenth of what Häkkinen did going down to the first corner, I'm sure I would have got a penalty,' he fumed. 'The rules are not the same for everybody in this business and I have become very nervous as a result.'

Senna suffered engine failure early on and Häkkinen ran confidently in the top four until he crashed coming out of the final corner, rumpling his McLaren quite badly against the guard rails but surviving intact without any physical damage. Despite this mishap, he remarked confidently: 'I have learned a lot of things and feel even stronger than I did at the end of last year.'

The penultimate race of the year was the Japanese Grand Prix at Suzuka, where Häkkinen finished a well-satisfied third. He dealt with the rapidly changing wet/dry track conditions like a veteran but, having thrown his MP4/8 off the road at Estoril the previous month, when he saw the 'P3' signal from his pit he was happy to settle for third. It was his first visit to the F1 victory podium. Quite clearly it would not be his last.

In the Australian Grand Prix Häkkinen got up to third place at one point, even though by this stage of the race he suspected that he was in serious trouble. 'Just before I made a stop for tyres, I felt the brakes getting softer,' he explained, 'and after the stop the problem became worse, the rears feeling soft while the front ones were locking up.'

Mika's stop dropped him to sixth before he trailed into the pits for good after 28 of the race's 79 laps. The caliper bridge pipe on the left rear brake was leaking and, after quick examination, the car was pushed away into its garage.

Mika finished the year 15th equal in the Drivers' World Championship solely on the strength of those four points scored at Suzuka. Considering he had raced in just three of the season's 16 races, it was not a bad achievement by anybody's standards.

And Häkkinen quickly proved, too, that he was a genuinely nice man, as McLaren team co-ordinator Jo Ramirez reflects. 'I like Mika's qualities of perseverance and the fact that he has stuck with it through thick and thin,' he reflects. 'He deserves to be there, right up at the front, getting the results now that the good times have returned.

'I remember when I met him for the first time, in Brazil back in 1992 by the hotel swimming pool, when he was driving for Lotus. A lot of young drivers tend to be cocky and over-confident, a bit full of themselves. But he was delightfully uncomplicated and up-front. He simply came over, introduced himself and quietly struck up a conversation, asking me how a big team like McLaren did things. I was very taken with him from the start.'

Make no mistake about it, Mika Häkkinen has brought a lot to the McLaren party. He arrived in his test driving role at the beginning of a season which saw Ayrton Senna and Michael Andretti paired together racing the Ford HB-engined MP4/8s. This was a crucial opportunity. Senna, suffused with a fit of the grumps because McLaren hadn't got a works engine deal that season, declined most invitations to test. Michael Andretti didn't quite know what he was about, struggling in what was to be a catastrophic F1 freshman year. So Mika had a clear run through as much testing as he wanted.

After Andretti was dropped by the team with three races to go, Mika found himself promoted to the race squad alongside Senna. Ramirez remembers that he ruffled Ayrton's feathers quite seriously when he qualified ahead of him at Estoril.

'When he beat the Big Man,' said Jo, 'Ayrton certainly wasn't amused. There were even a few remarks like, "Oh yes, and how many Grands Prix have you won?" when they were exchanging information in the de-briefs. But I think Senna was impressed.'

For all that, losing Senna at the end of 1993 was a major blow for the team. It needed an established lead driver and, to this end, Ron Dennis began to send out feelers towards Alain Prost. He wanted to discern whether or not the Frenchman might be available. Had he really been ready to retire after winning that fourth World Championship for Williams? Or was it just the threat of Senna's presence in that team which prompted him to hang up his helmet?

Prost was clearly wavering. He tested the McLaren–Peugeot MP4/9 at Estoril – and then decided that he would stay retired. The new car was not really up to competitive scratch, and he didn't want to damage his reputation. Some might have felt that the veteran Frenchman was not ready for a scrap at the wheel of a car which wasn't obviously front-running material when Senna would clearly be starting 1994 in a very strong position with the Williams FW16. Either way, he passed up the opportunity.

Much of the McLaren–Peugeot pre-race testing was carried out in relatively cool conditions which, most unfortunately, served to mask the threshold beyond which the French V10 engine began to be hampered by severe overheating. It was, the team soon discovered, a pretty temperamental engine, far from the 'bolt-in-and-go' experience which the team had enjoyed with the previous year's Cosworth V8.

'At McLaren there was no compromise in terms of the effort they put into their racing,' said Häkkinen frankly. 'I had to be very optimistic and hope that we would eventually reach a situation in 1994 from which we could win races.

'Yet we had to acknowledge that we simply did not have the power to get pole position and needed to spend much of the season concentrating on reliability. We just had to get to understand the problems and fix them.'

When it was clear that Prost would not be joining the team, Dennis signed up the British driver Martin Brundle to drive for them. Mika liked the British driver, but was under no illusions that he himself was quicker than Martin. Significantly quicker.

One factor behind that speed came, in Mika's view, from his left-foot braking technique. 'You can brake later and get on the power earlier with this approach,' he insisted. 'It could be worth a couple of tenths of a second a lap and, over a full race distance, that can add up to a really worthwhile amount.

'Yet it is not simply the time benefit, but also the fact that you are balancing yourself more comfortably in the car. It's basically like skiing, you feel everything that is going on with the car – cornering forces, braking. Your whole body feels in balance.'

The early-season third place at Imola on the wretched day of Senna's fatal accident boosted Mika's morale early on during the 1994 season, and he also looked on course for a place on the rostrum at Barcelona until a cracked water radiator precipitated another major engine failure. Then at Monaco came his golden moment, when he qualified the McLaren MP4/9 on the front row alongside Michael Schumacher's pole position Benetton – only to throw all his efforts away with a silly first-corner collision with Damon Hill's fast-starting Williams.

A mid-season slump inevitably caused Mika's morale to suffer, and he was most unfortunate to be at the centre of a first-corner multiple collision just after the start of the German Grand Prix at Hockenheim. The Finn had qualified eighth and was attempting to squeeze ahead of some rivals to gain track advantage. In hugging the pit wall, he started to squeeze David Coulthard's Williams out towards Mark Blundell's Tyrrell. Then chaos erupted as Mika suddenly found himself snapping broadside and shooting across the nose of his rivals, ending up hard against the barrier on the outside of the corner. In his wake, the pack scattered in all directions.

As Blundell also speared off the road, both Jordans found themselves with nowhere to go but into the gravel, along with the Sauber of Heinz-Harald Frentzen which had been clipped by the English driver's Tyrrell. Also eliminated in a haze of gravel and dust were Pierluigi Martini's Minardi and Johnny Herbert in his Lotus–Honda, knocked out by Häkkinen's team-mate Martin Brundle in the other McLaren.

Häkkinen was found guilty of precipitating this unfortunate incident. He was already racing under a suspended one-race ban which had been imposed by the FIA World Council for a rule infringement at Silverstone, and following a protracted stewards' inquiry this suspension was now activated, which meant he would be obliged to miss the Hungarian Grand Prix.

Legend has it that, walking back across the paddock at Hockenheim after Ron Dennis had offered the stewards an eloquent defence of his first-lap driving tactics, Mika turned to his employer and said: 'Bloody hell, Ron, you did such a good job in there that even I began to believe that it wasn't my fault.'

Frenchman Philippe Alliot, a Peugeot nominee, stood in for Häkkinen while he sat out the following race at Budapest. Returning to the McLaren–Peugeot cockpit at Spa-Francorchamps, Mika celebrated with his best F1 result yet: second place to Damon Hill's Williams FW16 in the Belgian Grand Prix.

Admittedly, Mika had crossed the line third and was promoted to the second step of the rostrum only after

Michael Schumacher's Benetton B194, the apparent victor, was disqualified after excessive wear was detected on its skid plate beneath the chassis. Nevertheless, it was a gratifying performance from the Finn, who started from eighth place on the grid.

Häkkinen was now fifth in the Drivers' Championship stakes with 14 points, finally rewarded with a long overdue dose of technical reliability from the Peugeot V10. There was more good fortune to come at Monza, where Mika stormed home third, moving up to within a single point of the fourth-placed Jean Alesi in the title battle. His team-mate Martin Brundle broadened the smile on Ron Dennis's face with a good run to fifth, strengthening the team's hold on fourth place in the Constructors' Championship table.

The Portuguese Grand Prix at Estoril produced another good result for the team. Häkkinen was again third, surging ahead of Alesi for fourth place in the drivers' table, while Brundle took sixth place. Yet another third place at Jerez was followed by seventh at Suzuka in the rain-soaked Japanese Grand Prix – but the season ended on a bitterly disappointing note with an accident in the final race in Adelaide.

Despite incurring a 10 second stop–go penalty for speeding in the pit lane, Häkkinen was running fourth with just four laps to go when the McLaren MP4/9 veered left into the concrete retaining wall under braking for the hairpin at the end of Brabham straight, the fastest part of the South Australian street circuit where the cars touch 190 mph.

The accident, which damaged the chassis of Mika's car quite badly, was officially attributed by the team to a possible braking problem. Strangely, Brundle – who finished a good third on his final outing as a McLaren team member – very nearly had a nasty accident on the slowing-down lap when his MP4/9's power steering packed up. His car veered sharply to the right, but he managed to keep it away from the wall.

For all that, at the end of the weekend Häkkinen could reflect on a gratifying first full season at McLaren. He had finished up fourth in the Drivers' Championship with 26 points, separating Ferrari drivers Gerhard Berger and Jean Alesi. For its part, McLaren had taken fourth place in the Constructors' Cup, comfortably ahead of Jordan but some way behind Ferrari.

Despite this more than respectable outcome, the McLaren–Peugeot alliance was coming to an end. Ron Dennis had judged that, long-term, this was not the way forward for his team. Instead, he decided to forge a new engine supply partnership with Mercedes-Benz, whose motorsport manager Norbert Haug had, in much the same way, concluded that the German car company needed a stronger F1 partner than the Swiss-based Sauber team.

This was a decision which would have a profound effect on everybody who worked for McLaren, in particular Mika Häkkinen. Ever since the great days of the Honda alliance, Ron Dennis had been seeking a route by means of which his team could return to a position of sustained success. Sustained success, mind you, was something more than just winning the occasional race. Dennis wanted McLaren to retake its former position as a power in the F1 land: a dominant force, not simply a competitive runner.

For Mercedes, the rationale was much the same. For a couple of years the famous German company had been hovering on the edge of a full-scale return to Formula One.

This reticence was not surprising. Mercedes had a proud racing heritage stretching back to the early years of the century, and its achievements in 1954/5 with the likes of Juan Manuel Fangio and Stirling Moss behind the wheel of its legendary W196 Grand Prix cars meant that the stakes were high: a return to F1 racing at any other than the highest level might jeopardize this unique image.

Moreover, the whole emphasis of F1 had changed beyond recognition since the mid-1950s. In those days the factory team at Mercedes' Stuttgart headquarters was entirely responsible for designing, engineering and manufacturing the cars and engines, in addition to funding and operating the entire racing team. Now things were very different. Mercedes's return to F1 in the 1990s was achieved by means of investing in British specialist engine builders Ilmor Engineering, which would later become a subsidiary of M-B itself. Sauber had been a competent partner, but lacked the potential to grow into a front-line team. McLaren, by contrast, fitted the bill to perfection.

'Being with McLaren put us under massive pressure,' recalled Ilmor co-founder Mario Illien. 'First of all, we were effectively changing ship halfway down the road towards designing and developing a new 3-litre engine. With that change [from Sauber to McLaren] came some changes in the idea of how we should best deal with the engine's "architecture" to deal with the new 50 mm stepped undertray regulations which were being introduced at the start of the 1995 season.'

As expected, Ilmor did a good job, building what was claimed to be the smallest, lightest and lowest F1 engine of its generation. Yet the task of integrating it into the chassis, endowing it with the requisite levels of driveability and generally developing the McLaren–Mercedes technical package into a winning concept, would take rather longer.

It was set to be a complicated year; yet nobody could have imagined just how complicated when the McLaren–Mercedes MP4/10 was officially unveiled at London's Science Museum. For Häkkinen, the season ahead looked like being a tricky one. By now he had the experience and ability to be regarded as an absolute number one in his own right; but pressure from McLaren's title sponsor Marlboro, the Philip Morris cigarette brand, dictated that an established star driver be signed up.

This pressure for a high-profile name resulted in the acquisition of Nigel Mansell. The veteran 40-year-old British driver had won the World Championship in 1992 at the wheel of a Williams before falling out with his employer and defecting to the US Indycar series as a result. He won the US series title in 1993, but the competitive form of his Newman Haas team Lola–Ford wobbled precariously in 1994, with the result that Mansell was only too willing to accept a guest driving role back at Williams after the tragic death of Ayrton Senna in the San Marino Grand Prix at Imola.

Williams had an option on Mansell's continued services in 1995, but eventually opted for the young Scot David Coulthard as a partner for Damon Hill. Marlboro fancied having Mansell in the McLaren–Mercedes squad, he was available and the deal was done. Häkkinen, it seemed, was about to be eclipsed.

In reality, however, the Mansell/McLaren alliance was always going to be a shaky affair. The McLaren–Mercedes MP4/10 was not the most obviously competitive car from the outset – and Mansell was at the stage in his career where he wanted a competitive car. His contemporary experience at Williams had left him with a very clear idea of what constituted a competitive F1 car and his body language at the end of his first test in the McLaren MP4/10 indicated very strongly that this car certainly did not fall into that category.

Suddenly, the advantage began to swing imperceptibly towards Häkkinen. The young and extremely ambitious Finn was still hungry, having yet to win his first Grand Prix. Mansell's competitive instincts burned as strongly as ever, but for him the time for doing battle in a mid-grid car had probably passed. He wanted to demonstrate his talent, but in a car that could run at the front from the outset.

Häkkinen, of course, had absolutely no intention of deferring to the Englishman. 'Nigel is a quick driver,' he acknowledged. 'He's been World Champion and he's been around for a long time. I'm ready for it, though. I'm interested to see what he's like to work with and I hope we can help each other.

'Everyone has different opinions of him, I know, but for me he's a very special driver, and of course my manager, Keke Rosberg, used to be his team-mate and tells me good things about him – but that was a long time ago.'

The real reason Marlboro wanted Mansell on the McLaren team strength was to force Häkkinen to raise the level of his game. They knew he could push even harder than they'd seen in 1994, but also recognized that Martin Brundle was not the man to put him under pressure. Mansell, they judged, would get that job done.

Unfortunately, the Mansell/McLaren alliance began to go wrong almost from the word go. When it came to his first seat

fitting in the McLaren MP4/10, Nigel complained that the
cockpit simply didn't offer sufficient elbow room to enable
him to steer properly. Therefore the team decided to build
him a revised monocoque, a process which in itself would
involve him missing the first two races of the season. In his
place, British driver Mark Blundell deputized as Häkkinen's
team-mate.

During those first two outings in Brazil and Argentina,
Mika quickly became accustomed to the MP4/10's short-
comings. In particular, it lacked front-end grip, a defect
aggravated by the explosive power curve of the Mercedes
V10, making the car doubly difficult to drive.

Mika began the year with a superb run to fourth place at
Interlagos, but at Buenos Aires he chopped across Eddie
Irvine's Jordan with an impact that left him with a punctured
rear tyre which sent him straight into the gravel trap.

Mansell's rebuilt chassis was ready after only 33 days, a
remarkable feat of redesigning and manufacturing on the
part of the McLaren team. Once back behind the wheel,
Nigel confirmed the other drivers' initial reservations about
lack of front-end grip. It was not the sort of car he felt happy
with, preferring an over-steering machine with much more
front-end bite. Still, when he finally drove his first race in the
car at Imola, he did his best; and, after a number of alarms
and excursions, he finished the San Marino Grand Prix in
tenth place, both he and Häkkinen having started with the
handicap of choosing slicks on a cold track which had only
just started to dry after heavy rain had fallen during the
morning. As things turned out, this was the only race which
Mansell would ever complete at the wheel of a McLaren–
Mercedes.

By contrast, Häkkinen drove notably well at Imola to bag a fine fifth – and he also proved stupendously quick on slicks while the track was still damp in the opening phase of the event. This performance which helped establish the Finn as de facto number one driver in the mind of the McLaren team personnel, however the situation might be perceived from the touchlines.

Then came the Spanish Grand Prix at Barcelona's Circuit de Catalunya. Häkkinen qualified ninth, just one place ahead of Mansell, but in the race it was a different matter. Mika ran comfortably ahead of the British driver, who eventually pulled into the pits to retire after 18 laps, following a lurid slide across a gravel trap. It was the end of the Mansell/McLaren relationship.

'It is quite clear that our performance here is inadequate for our own objectives,' said Ron Dennis, picking his words with some care. 'Whatever the capabilities of our car, we haven't exploited it yet. In final qualifying we clearly went in the wrong direction.

'This track highlights our car's deficiencies in long, sweeping curves. The problem is also exaggerated by characteristics of the engine in a certain rev range, but it is mainly the car. We should be sixth and seventh on the grid, but at the moment we don't have a car capable of taking on the lead Benetton, the two Williams and the Ferraris.

'There is only way to remove these problems and that is hard work, nothing else. There is no magic in motor racing – it's all numbers and understanding what the car and drivers require. And getting on with it.'

A few days after the Spanish debacle, Dennis journeyed to Mansell's home in the West Country, close to the Woodbury Golf and Country Club which had increasingly become the focal point of the British driver's business life over the preceding 12 months. 'Extensive and open discussions' were reported by both parties, and they decided to dissolve their partnership.

That meant that the popular Mark Blundell was again recruited to drive at Monaco, where he finished in fifth place on a day which saw Häkkinen posted as an early retirement with engine failure. This was followed by a disappointing Canadian Grand Prix for Mika when his McLaren was eliminated in a first-lap collision with Johnny Herbert's Benetton.

There were some close to the team who, by this stage in the season, were starting to harbour private reservations about Mika's potential. The raw speed was certainly there, but he seemed to be having difficulty coming to terms with the complicated and challenging technical situation in which the McLaren team found itself during the 1995 season. Making a meaningful contribution to the process of developing a Grand Prix car seemed, at times, to be almost more than he could manage.

A lacklustre seventh place in the French Grand Prix at Magny-Cours was followed with disappointing retirements at both Silverstone and Hockenheim. Then the engine failed after only three laps at Budapest and he spun off early in the Belgian Grand Prix at Spa-Francorchamps – a slight lapse of which the McLaren team took a relaxed view as they acknowledged that on this occasion he had been caught out by the Mercedes engine's somewhat abrupt power delivery.

At Monza, at least, the race produced some welcome relief from Häkkinen's run of misfortune, even though practice and qualifying seemed to be unfolding in the usual manner. On Friday Mika left the road on two occasions, freely admitting that he'd made a mistake first time round which left the entire left-hand suspension wiped off his McLaren MP4/10B. However, after the second such apparent lapse – which ruined his first qualifying bid – the team admitted that it was 95 per cent likely that the failure of a steering component had caused the crash. Eventually he qualified eighth, but drove superbly on the Sunday afternoon to finish second behind Johnny Herbert's Benetton, admittedly benefiting from a high level of retirements due to incidents among the established front runners but at least keeping himself decisively away from involvement in any such episodes.

Sadly, this was only a brief respite from the McLaren team's run of deeply disappointing results. In the Portuguese Grand Prix at Estoril, Mika again failed to make it to the finish due to engine failure, while an eighth place two laps behind Schumacher's winning Benetton B195 made the European Grand Prix at the Nürburgring – in front of a grandstand full of Mercedes corporate guests – another embarrassment which Mika and McLaren could have well done without. A combination of handling problems and difficulties getting the tyres warmed up to optimum operating temperatures was judged to be the cause of the problem, but it did little for morale.

Häkkinen had to miss the Pacific Grand Prix at the TI Aida circuit in Japan after being hospitalized for an appendix operation, and the team's young Danish test driver Jan Magnussen stood in for the absent regular driver. When Mika returned to the cockpit at Suzuka, he qualified superbly to take third place on the grid for the Japanese Grand Prix and in the race itself stormed home to take second place behind Schumacher.

This was a great morale-boosting performance for the entire team, but at Adelaide during first qualifying for the Australian Grand Prix it seemed that Mika's career might have abruptly come to an end. After a sudden deflation of its left rear tyre, caused by running over debris on the circuit, Häkkinen's McLaren MP4/10 crashed very heavily into a single row of tyres facing a concrete barrier on the 110 mph, fourth-gear right-hand corner leading out on to the Brabham Straight.

By any standards this was a truly horrifying impact; and, as the session was red-flagged to a halt, that ominous, almost self-conscious silence which inevitably attends any sporting disaster seemed to settle over the pits and paddock. First indications were that it was bad. Very bad.

Only later would it become clear that Mika's life was saved in the immediate aftermath of the impact by the prompt and efficient intervention of the marshals at the scene and the doctors who rushed quickly to his aid. His head was held straight to prevent him from choking on his own blood and a tracheotomy was performed at the trackside to prevent him suffering possible brain damage through loss of oxygen. Only when his condition was stable was he transferred to the Royal Victoria Hospital in Adelaide, where his recovery would duly be monitored by the FIA medical delegate Professor Sid Watkins.

Professor Watkins admitted that an airbag could possibly have saved Häkkinen from sustaining such a serious injury. 'We are not sure whether his helmet struck the steering wheel or the side of the cockpit,' he added, 'but we will study the in-car camera tape in slow motion to reach a conclusion.'

He added that technical research on airbags for F1 applications was under way. 'We are working to determine the optimum size and shape and the best site in which to place it in an F1 car,' he explained.

'The technology to inflate the bag in the time required is available, but, following its inflation, we need to control the rate at which it deflates so that the bag will not obstruct the cockpit or interfere with the extrication or escape of the driver.' At the time of writing, four years after Häkkinen's lucky escape, airbags have yet to appear on F1 cars.

The 24 hours immediately following the accident were stressful for everybody close to Mika Häkkinen. It soon became clear that he was out of danger, yet it would be a few more days before everybody was certain he had suffered no permanent physical impairment. Unspoken at the time, there was inevitably some speculation over whether or not he would ever race again, but this was an issue which would take weeks, if not months, finally to resolve.

# Chapter Four

# After Adelaide

The McLaren team closed ranks around its favourite son. Ron Dennis and his wife Lisa were regular and attentive visitors to Mika's bedside, and his girlfriend Erja flew out from Europe to be with him. For the next few months they nursed him, shielded him from the media and kept the pressure away from him. Happily, his physical recovery did not take too long. But the worry remained that there might be psychological scars which would take longer to heal.

At the start of the 1996 season Häkkinen looked shaky and unsure of himself. His strained eyes were hidden behind dark glasses; his naturally pale complexion looked pallid, his facial expression strained. Sure enough, he was quick first time out of the box when it came to testing the new McLaren MP4/11, but he later confessed that he felt a streak of genuine apprehension when he accelerated out on to the Paul Ricard circuit for his first private test since the accident. This, he explained, was not so much a question of lack of confidence in his ability to drive competitively as a doubt whether he might be inhibited by memories of the Adelaide accident. In the event, it all went well. He felt a few moments of concern, but was soon back into the swing of things. He was certainly on his way back. But could McLaren provide him with a winning car?

A young Häkkinen considers abandoning the troubled Lotus team and joining the circus. Fortunately a seat at McLaren came along…

*Above*, Mika joined Lotus with an impressive CV and scored points in only his third Grand Prix. *Below*, Ron Dennis *(right)* offered him job as reserve driver at McLaren in 1993.

*Opposite top*, he was leading the team by the start of 1994 and knocking on the door of success by the time McLaren and Mercedes got up to speed in 1997 *(opposite below)*

*Above*, silver dream racer: the 1998 season saw highs, such as a truly dominant performance 'at home' in Monaco *(below)*, and lows such as Spa where he clashed with Schumacher at the start *(opposite top)*. But at Suzuka *(opposite below)* the World Championship was finally his.

*Above*, Mika with his wife Erja, who nursed him back to health after his near-fatal accident at Adelaide in 1995. They married three years later.

*Below*, the McLaren team celebrates winning both drivers' and constructors' titles in 1998, ending a period in the wilderness which began when Senna left the team in 1993.

*Above*, the defending champion patiently awaits the start in Austria, one of several races in 1999 when the odds seemed stacked against him.

*Right*, distraught at Monza: Häkkinen had the 1999 Italian Grand Prix seemingly in his pocket when a simple gear change error pitched him off the road and out of the race.

After a difficult season Mika held it all together brilliantly at Suzuka to dominate the race and win his second consecutive drivers' title. His chief rival that year – in Schumacher's enforced absence – was Eddie Irvine *(above)* who was gracious in defeat. *Below*, celebrating with McLaren chief Ron Dennis.

Much was expected in the second season of the McLaren–Mercedes alliance. The Mansell episode was now put firmly behind them and the popular Scottish driver David Coulthard, who had won the 1995 Portuguese Grand Prix for Williams, was recruited as Häkkinen's team-mate. On the technical side, while the latest McLaren–Mercedes MP4/11 represented a definite technical turn for the better, it also fell short of the team's expectations to some considerable degree.

Make no mistake, an enormous amount of detailed effort was expended on the MP4/11. To start with, there was a minuscule 7.5 per cent 'rollover' of components into the new car, and when Häkkinen duly posted the fastest time at the final pre-season Estoril test, there was no doubt that the car represented a major improvement.

Mika was also quick to report that the latest version of the Mercedes V10 represented a significant improvement. It had run on the dynamometer only a week before the MP4/11 enjoyed its maiden test outing, and Mika was happy to discern an appreciable improvement in the engine's mid-range torque characteristics. It was softer, less abrupt in its response. But Ilmor had also set itself the target of boosting its performance by 5 per cent, a goal that was more than welcome to the drivers.

By the time Mika lined up fifth on the starting grid for the first Australian Grand Prix to be held at Melbourne's Albert Park circuit, a spate of irritating piston problems had been corrected and the car ran reliably. Fifth on the grid seemed quite respectable on the face of it, but it was a full 1.6 seconds away from F1 debutant Jacques Villeneuve's pole time in the Williams–Renault.

This was an unusually large margin to be separating the first five cars on any contemporary F1 starting grid, and Mika was a little frustrated that the MP4/11 had apparently lost some of the crisp response which had so impressed him at the Estoril test. 'I have come here to win, not to finish fifth,' he growled after the final times were published.

Come the race itself, at least Mika proved he could last the full distance without any physical problems. He drove a measured race into fifth place, although both the McLaren–Mercedes were fitted with extra oil tank capacity on the evening before the race as a precautionary measure. As it turned out, Mika was the only McLaren driver to complete the course: Coulthard's maiden race for the team ended with a stuck throttle.

Over the bumps at São Paulo's Interlagos circuit, Mika and David found themselves battling for grip in the second round of the title chase, the Brazilian Grand Prix. Mika managed to qualify seventh – good enough in a sense, for he split the two much-fancied Benettons of Jean Alesi and Gerhard Berger – but he found himself struggling for balance for much of the time.

In the race, pouring rain came to his assistance and he barnstormed his way into fourth place, also ending the day fourth in the Drivers' World Championship table. Coulthard, by contrast, had a bad time and spun into retirement on the treacherous track surface. Already Mika was gently, unobtrusively, reminding everybody that he still regarded himself as team leader, even though McLaren held to its formal commitment to equal status between its two drivers as the admirable cornerstone of its *modus operandi*.

Yet the McLaren MP4/11 still could not be regarded as a front-line machine. In that connection, a twist of mischievous irony was delivered by rival team owner Ken Tyrrell after the first few races of the '96 season. Asked what his team's underlying ambition for the year was, he fired back instantly: 'To beat McLaren.'

Then he added, with a definite twinkle in his eye: 'But I suppose we're not aiming very high!'

Such knockabout humour might not have been appreciated in the boardroom of McLaren International (or of Mercedes-Benz, come to that) during the early months of 1996. In fact, anyone trying to run that statement past Ron Dennis would almost certainly be fixed with a glance which would turn them to stone.

Yet even Ron might have acknowledged that there was a serious sub-text underlying Tyrrell's apparently jocular observation. And, as the Anglo-German alliance went into the European GP at the Nürburgring – a quarter of the way through the year's championship battle – the partners were working even harder than ever to produce a decisive upsurge in performance as the calendar settled down to its relentless fortnightly grind.

In particular, the team was aiming to exorcise memories of its lamentable performance in the previous October's European Grand Prix. Mark Blundell recalled that race as the 'only time he had burst out laughing at the wheel of a racing car'. The realization that his McLaren had been overtaken by a Pacific driven by Jean-Denis Deletraz was almost too much for him to comprehend.

Yet putting a finger on the problem had not been a straightforward matter. McLaren remained a team with a strong belief in its own technical competence. 'We work very hard with much higher levels of data than are available to our opposition,' said Dennis confidently at Buenos Aires, as he attempted to analyse the MP4/11 qualifying performance.

Still, however, Häkkinen and Coulthard lacked the sort of confidence in their car's front-end grip which enables a driver to pitch into a corner knowing precisely where the nose will go. This was much the same accusation as that Mika had levelled at the previous year's MP4/10B and critics inevitably wondered whether the current difficulty should have really come as a surprise. With the exception of some input by Steve Nichols, relatively late in the day, the McLaren design team had remained essentially unchanged for the past three seasons or more.

Dennis had never been a man to deal emotionally with his problems. He has always maintained that 'there is no magic' to achieving success in F1. Technical snags, he maintains, can ultimately be broken down into bite-sized chunks – minced morsels, if you like – and solved in a logical and progressive manner. Yet reversing the MP4/11's initially disappointing form clearly remained a complex conundrum for his engineers.

Having Alain Prost aboard as a member of the McLaren technical team certainly offered some worthwhile pointers. After Jean Alesi ran race laps almost a full two seconds quicker than Coulthard in Buenos Aires – having been barely a second quicker in qualifying – Prost trenchantly reiterated the view that there was no way that the McLaren was fundamentally two seconds slower than a Benetton.

Alain also confirmed that the latest 'Phase 3' version of the Ilmor-built Mercedes V10 was continually improving as far as driveability was concerned. Top-end performance did not seem to be a problem. It was also clear that Mercedes' motivation to give McLaren as much support as possible remained unshakeable, although it did not require a clairvoyant to point out that the Stuttgart management was not satisfied with the level of success achieved to date.

It was also particularly interesting that the rest of the F1 fraternity was watching McLaren's progress with something approaching a sense of bewilderment. There was an underlying feeling that the team would rise again to win races, but whether the nature of F1 would ever allow the McLaren–Mercs to dominate as the McLaren–Hondas had seemed open to debate.

'I don't want to comment about McLaren,' said one well-known driver who perhaps felt he has might have a possible future with the team. 'Taking a cheap shot might give me some short-term satisfaction, but it would result in too much long-term aggravation.'

John Watson, himself a former McLaren F1 driver who was dropped by Dennis at the end of 1983, thought that McLaren would definitely win races again. 'But probably not until 1997 if we are talking about winning from the front,' he mused. 'If they win this year, it will probably only be through luck.' Prescient words indeed.

Tyrrell engineering director Harvey Postlethwaite offered some thoughts. 'One of the obvious problems is that the difference between cars is often dependent on the parts you cannot see,' he noted enigmatically. 'But looking at the McLaren I must say I wonder whether they've quite understood what 1996 cars are all about.'

Despite this, Dennis and his colleagues could take heart from one historical statistic. Williams was into its third season with Renault before it established itself as a consistent winning force in 1991. Even so, the team scored three lucky wins in 1989/90, usually when the all-conquering McLaren–Hondas encountered some sort of problems.

When it came down to it, nobody doubted that McLaren and Mercedes possessed the raw ingredients to produce a winning recipe. They were also, in the words of a key team member, 'working, working, working, like the craziest people in the world'. But equally, there was no doubt that the cooks were not getting the job done. No matter how the team sliced it, all the evidence available to outsiders suggested a significant shortcoming in the way in which the team's design and engineering department was operating.

Historically, F1 teams have thrived on decisive technical leadership. Engineers like Patrick Head, Ross Brawn and Gary Anderson are invested with considerable operational autonomy. What they say goes as far as the technical side of their teams are concerned.Nobody was saying that McLaren's design and engineering staff was useless. It just seemed to lack the sort of forceful, unchallenged and dictatorial leadership which Ron Dennis had for so long imposed on the commercial side of the operation. Some said this reflected admirably on Dennis's sense of personal loyalty to key employees. Others concluded that it was simply an unwillingness on the part of the McLaren boss to fire the wrong guy without what he regarded as sufficient proof of his deficiencies.

On the driving side things were much better. In Mika Häkkinen and David Coulthard McLaren unquestionably had two of the most accomplished drivers in the F1 community; yet both men unexpectedly found themselves fighting for their reputations as the 1996 season unfolded.

Mika was no longer a driver with time on his side. He was now in his fifth season of F1 and long overdue for his first victory. He surely had to win at least one race in 1996 to retain not only his confidence, but also his market value. If he did not, people speculated, then he might have to think about switching teams for 1997.

For Coulthard, who had scored his first Grand Prix victory at Estoril the previous September in only his first full F1 season, the problem was less pressing, even though he had initially been slower than Häkkinen in practice and qualifying.

Häkkinen remained a loyal and committed McLaren team player. After Melbourne, he had said: 'I really don't want to put the team down and suggest the car is junk. Technically it is excellent, I think, and a huge amount of work has gone into it. The engineers have made a terrific effort over the winter and it's just a question of getting the best out of the car.'

Yet there was no concealing his abject frustration with both his qualifying and race performance at Buenos Aires. When he remarked, 'The car is not good enough, but not far away,' he was unconsciously stating the obvious. Being not far away is simply not anywhere near good enough in an era when Williams and Benetton have made a virtual monopoly of the winning business.

Coulthard also remained commendably resilient and did a good job in retaining an analytical approach to the MP4/11 problems. 'Despite all our work on the chassis, I think it is still aerodynamically sensitive,' he said thoughtfully.

'It pitches around, making it difficult to get into a corner in a consistent fashion. But we think we have an understanding of this characteristic and McLaren have the resources to make the necessary changes.'

Was he depressed about the way things had developed in the first three races? 'Not depressed,' he replied firmly. 'No, never. Disappointed in the car's lack of response, which does not seem totally logical. I will admit that it was a new experience to be lapped by the two Williams in Melbourne, but I haven't suddenly become a bad driver overnight.'

Coulthard had another chance to gain the upper hand over Häkkinen in the fourth round of the '96 title chase at the Nürburgring. The Scot qualified sixth, three places ahead of his team-mate, and stormed through to third in the race. Sadly, this promising showing was not mirrored by Häkkinen. The Finn had been running third when he came in for his first refuelling stop at the end of lap 25. Unfortunately, the fast approach to the Nürburgring pit lane caused him to exceed the speed limit. That meant he had to come back in six laps later to take a 10 second stop–go penalty which dropped him down to sixth place. He then exceeded the speed limit again coming in for his second refuelling stop, earning a fourth visit to the pits for a second stop–go penalty. Mika wound up an extremely frustrated eighth at the end of the day, feeling perhaps that there was something wrong with the pit lane speed limiter mechanism on his car. A detailed check revealed nothing amiss, however, so he just had to grin and bear it.

However, in general terms, the McLaren team came away from the European Grand Prix feeling a degree of measured satisfaction. A major step forward had been made on the MP4/11 chassis set-up and a revised inlet system on the Mercedes V10 engine had considerably enhanced the engine's driveability. The car had also been quick on the straights during practice and qualifying, although this was largely attributable to the fact that they were running with minimal downforce.

Even so, a quick glance at the Constructors' Championship table after four races indicated that the team still had a long way to go. Williams now led on 55 points with McLaren only fourth, having accumulated a measly nine points. Not good.

The San Marino Grand Prix was not good for Häkkinen either. Coulthard qualified fourth, but Mika was down in 11th at the end of the crucial hour-long session. He wasn't at all happy with the handling balance of his car and punctuated his efforts with a quick spin on the tight right-hander before the pits.

Come the race, Coulthard vaulted ahead into an immediate lead which he held until his first refuelling stop on lap19. He eventually had to retire with hydraulic problems after 44 laps, but up to that point had run consistently strongly in the top three. Häkkinen, by contrast, was bogged down in slower traffic from the outset – the legacy of that lowly grid position – and had another exasperatingly frustrating outing, collecting yet another stop-go penalty and then suffering an engine failure on the last lap while he was running seventh.

On reflection, the early summer of 1996 represented the lowest ebb of what could be described as Häkkinen's front-line F1 career to date. Injuries aside, he seemed to have been wrong-footed by Coulthard's presence in the team. Moreover, events which would unfold at Monaco left one or two McLaren insiders frustrated beyond belief at his performance in the additional race-morning warm-up which was provided to acclimatize the competitors to the wet conditions.

Having again been outqualified by Coulthard – fifth to seventh – Mika set the pace in this extra 15-minute session, only completely to destroy his McLaren MP4/11 in a huge accident at Tabac. 'He was running three seconds a lap faster than anyone else on the track,' shrugged McLaren team coordinator Jo Ramirez. 'I just don't understand what he was thinking about.'

Come the race, Coulthard finished a strong second. Mika seemed to be on his way to fifth when he found himself involved in a bizarre last-lap accident. Eddie Irvine, having pirouetted his Ferrari, spun-turned his way back into the race at the Portier corner just as Häkkinen arrived on the scene. Mika had no option but to run into the back of the slowing Ferrari; then, to add insult to injury, his Finnish arch-rival Mika Salo slammed into the back of the McLaren. The threesome was now left in the surreal situation of being locked together, stationary, out on the circuit. Small wonder that Mika almost kicked his McLaren in abject frustration in the process of vacating its cockpit.

With six of the year's races completed, the 1996 season was not looking a great deal better than the previous one as far as Häkkinen was concerned. Damon Hill was apparently surging away with the Drivers' World Championship, having amassed 43 points at this stage of the season to Jacques Villeneuve's 22. Mika was stuck in tenth place on six points, and his task was made doubly frustrating by the fact that even Coulthard had amassed ten points, the Scot marking himself out as the superior McLaren partner in several events.

The story of the 1996 season would be one of technical snakes and ladders for the McLaren–Mercedes team. They were convinced that they were on the trail of the technical solutions which would result in a consistent upsurge in form. Yet short-term inconsistency seemed to be playing too prominent a role in their performances. Just as they inched forward up the ladder towards better times, suddenly – and sometimes without any rhyme or reason – they would find themselves plunging back down the snake and having to repeat the painstaking groundwork. It was a frustrating time.

Second place for Coulthard at Monaco might have been gratifying enough, but the next race at Barcelona left both David and Mika struggling throughout the weekend. Qualifying for the Spanish Grand Prix at least saw Mika out-run his team-mate, but 10th and 14th respectively in the line-up was hardly calculated to fill everybody with optimism.

The long straights and high-speed corners at the Circuit de Catalunya seemed to be placing heavy demands on the McLarens' aerodynamic package and they were certainly found to be lacking. Not only were the cars difficult to balance out, they pattered unnervingly over the circuit's high-frequency bumps.

Race day was marred by torrential rain, allowing Michael Schumacher to run away to a commanding victory in his Ferrari F310. Coulthard was eliminated in a multiple pile-up accelerating away from the starting grid, leaving Mika to trail home an uncertain and rather tentative fifth, lapped by the winner before the chequered flag.

McLaren stayed on at Barcelona for another intensive round of testing immediately after the race. More than 2,000 km was covered by two cars which amounted to more than two Grand Prix distances per day for three days. Interestingly,

Mika was rested for this test and the driving duties were shared out between Coulthard and development drivers Alain Prost and Jan Magnussen.

All this effort was backed up by a redoubled effort from Mercedes-Benz, which carried out a huge amount of work on its transient dynamometers at Stuttgart in an effort to improve the engine's driveability. Häkkinen was quite impressed with the feel of the car when he returned to the cockpit for qualifying at Montreal, lining up to start the Canadian Grand Prix just 0.7 seconds behind Damon Hill's pole position Williams.

'Sixth is satisfying, but being seven-tenths away from pole position is still too much,' said the Finn. 'The circuit traditionally has a very low grip level and it is difficult to achieve lap times which are as good as we would have liked.'

In the race, Coulthard and Häkkinen ran in close company, with Mika staying ahead until he locked his rear brakes and spun at the hairpin while lapping Giancarlo Fisichella's Minardi. They wound up fourth and fifth, reasonable enough under the circumstances, although Mika admitted that he should have stayed in front.

Aerodynamic improvements were now coming through the McLaren development system thick and fast as the 1996 season approached its midway point. Pre-race testing at Magny-Cours in preparation for the French Grand Prix really raised everybody's hopes as Mika was right on the pace during testing and qualified fifth within a second of Schumacher's pole-winning Ferrari. Mika reported that the car's pitch sensitivity – that's to say, its inclination towards sudden fore/aft handling changes in response to acceleration and braking – was much reduced.

The car was nicer to drive, but minor gremlins meant that Mika could not improve on fifth in the race, one place ahead of Coulthard. Häkkinen was frustrated by an acute gear-change problem, losing the use of first and second gears at around the lap 30 mark, while Coulthard reported that his car was too stiffly set up for the conditions.

Third and fifth in the British Grand Prix at Silverstone followed this result, with Mika making what must have seemed a rare visit to the rostrum. The MP4/11s were still very nervous on the high-speed corners, but handled well on the slow infield loop section. Häkkinen again qualified fourth for the German Grand Prix at Hockenheim, but succumbed to gearbox problems after only 13 laps, leaving Coulthard to finish a distant fifth.

A lapped fourth place in the Hungarian Grand Prix was not much for Mika to write home about, although it was a result which carried McLaren to within a point of rivals Benetton in the contest for third place in the Constructors' Championship.

During the run-up to the Hungarian race, McLaren threw another fascinating straw into the F1 wind by testing Ralf Schumacher, the 21-year-old younger brother of Ferrari ace Michael, in one of their cars at Silverstone. There was a test driving job on offer at McLaren for 1997; but, although Ralf said it was his 'target to sit in a McLaren next year', he would eventually opt to race for the Jordan–Peugeot squad.

Häkkinen was back on the rostrum again at Spa-Francorchamps, thanks to a strong third place in the Belgian Grand Prix; but it was at Monza that Mika demonstrated that there was now genuine winning potential to be obtained both from himself and from the McLaren–Mercedes partnership.

Running third in the opening phase of the race, he damaged the nose section of his car after a tyre was flipped into his path by Jean Alesi's Benetton. The kerbs at Monza had been heavily revised for this race and, after complaints from the drivers about the potential damage they threatened to the underside of their cars, tyre barriers were placed on the edge of the chicanes to minimize the chances of anybody taking an expensive short cut.

After this incident Häkkinen had to come into the pits for repairs, resuming 17th, but then stormed back to third at the chequered flag, winding up only 48 seconds behind Schumacher's victorious Ferrari despite that stop. Without that unscheduled delay, Mika could certainly have been counted a potential winner.

Even so, the last two races of the season highlighted yet again just how unpredictably the McLaren drivers' fortunes had ebbed and flowed throughout the season. The Portuguese Grand Prix at Estoril was surely their most embarrassing moment of the year, with Mika inadvertently running into the back of David, spinning his team-mate over the kerb while at the same time knocking off his own nose section. Mika had to call it a day as a result of this collision, while David trailed home 13th. Still, McLaren now had 45 points in the Constructors' table, and with Ferrari and Benetton respectively nine and ten points ahead with only a single race left to run, it would not take a miracle for Ron Dennis's team to improve on fourth place.

Häkkinen finished third in the Japanese Grand Prix, rounding off the season with fifth place in the Drivers' World Championship. At the end of the season, in the *Autocourse* annual, I wrote:

*The McLaren MP4/11 was at its best in low-downforce, fast-circuit configuration and Mika's peerless car control could be guaranteed to get the best out of it in these circumstances. He drove a potentially winning race at Monza, recovering from 17th to third after an early delay to change a damaged nose wing.*

*Despite failing to win a single race, Mika and McLaren reaffirmed their confidence in each other by concluding a new contract for the 1997 season. There is a mutual regard and affection between driver and team which inclined both partners to continue the relationship. Even so, it is now three years since Ayrton Senna scored McLaren's last Grand Prix victory and Mika now has more than five seasons' racing experience in F1. Next year both must deliver. No more excuses are acceptable.*

There were people in the F1 business who believed that Mika Häkkinen's career was effectively written off. Sure, he had recovered from the trauma of the injuries sustained in Adelaide; but he certainly didn't look the same man. Gone was the easy, open demeanour, replaced instead by a slightly strained and preoccupied look. His eyes, apparently extremely sensitive to light, were usually hidden from view behind dark glasses. Initially, he looked like a man who was struggling to keep his spirits up.

'I think it is a little difficult to pinpoint precisely when I felt totally better,' he reflected much later. 'I don't think there was a single day when I got up in the morning and felt, "Right, I'm my old self again." It was a more gradual process. What you have to remember is that Formula One is a very athletic sport and you have to sustain a high level of fitness throughout the season.

'My problem was that, after I was released from hospital in Adelaide, I spent a long time at home without doing any training. Then when the doctors finally gave me permission to start my training programme again, I suddenly realized all through that time of inaction I had been losing a degree of my mental performance.

'I was really quite down, so when the season started I was faced with the challenge of both making progress with my body and my mental state. I was certainly not 100 per cent in Melbourne, but every day I steadily felt better, and the business of driving was causing me no problem.'

Häkkinen admits that he was obviously slightly disappointed about the performance of the McLaren MP4/11 in the early races of the year. 'I had worked enormously hard to regain my fitness,' he explained, 'and I came back to racing hoping that I would be able to challenge for race wins from the outset.

'As a consequence, when we found we were only in a position to run in the region of fifth or sixth place, it was a disappointment. These were not the results I wanted and, by Imola and Monaco, it became clear that I was not really performing at my best.

'I had to think through all the problems, because much of the trouble was with me rather than the car. The fact of the matter was that I was trying to work so hard on specific areas of the car's performance that I had somehow lost sight of the overall picture.

'Eventually I had to sit down with the engineers and agree that I should concentrate as much as possible on the business of driving while they spent their time working on the cars. At Monaco, for the team, things started to change for the better, and by the time we got to Silverstone I believed we were making really firm progress. Yet everybody in this business knows very well that it just doesn't matter whether you are third or fourth. Winning is the only thing anybody wants to hear about.'

Such a remark naturally led to speculation that Mika might be considering a change of teams in 1997. One sensed that he has an enormous loyalty to McLaren, but he dodged the enquiry. 'Okay, yes, I do feel a member of the McLaren family,' he admitted. 'But Keke and Ron Dennis have not yet sat down to discuss things.'

He would not comment on suggestions that he would like to switch to the Williams team, should the opportunity permit, nor would he comment on speculation that he could not agree with Ron Dennis on the size of a retainer for 1997. However, he was generous in his praise of the McLaren–Mercedes package.

'The engine has made fantastic progress over the last four races,' he explained. 'Every aspect is better. Power, driveability and torque. Everything just works properly – although I have to confess that I don't know what a Renault V10 is like.

'McLaren is a fantastic team. Like me, they are not new boys to this business, but we are all going in the right direction. The plans and commitment both McLaren and Mercedes have for the future are 100 per cent and I am totally confident in their ability to get the job done and win races.'

Mika was now settled with his Finnish girlfriend Erja in Monaco, where he had come to enjoy the temperate year-round climate. 'I remember being amazed when I lived in England for a while in my Formula Three days,' he recalled. 'Although it is often very cold there, the houses are not really adapted for the conditions!

'At least in Finland all the house have double glazing and good central heating. The climate in Monaco is ideal and I can train outdoors even in winter. It is also convenient for travelling. It takes ages to get to a Grand Prix from Finland, while from here it is easy. Keke also lives here, I have a circle of friends and there are so many celebrities in town that one more makes no difference so that people leave you alone to get on with your life.'

During the summer of 1996 Mika had no doubts that he still retained the motivation to attack every race weekend with the same optimism and commitment. 'I still enjoy driving an F1 car as much as ever,' he says. 'If I didn't, I would stop.

'There are moments when you feel very low and your motivation slips, but you just have to pull yourself up together and start again. Driving has brought me so much, and I don't just mean material things. Sometimes when I am pushing to the limit in qualifying, I feel as though I am flying above it watching myself at work in the cockpit.

'I don't feel I have missed out on my youth by devoting myself to this sport. I enjoy my life and my driving and most of my friends would give anything to be in my shoes.'

# Chapter Five

# The big time

'Again, it was one of those things you couldn't have done if it wasn't Ron. I doubt I would have dared to do it with anyone else. Negotiating contracts is always difficult, we are not always on the same side. But the best sign is that Mika is going into his fifth season with the team at a time when McLaren hasn't been having the best time.

'McLaren has the ability to get back to the top, although I'm now saying this for the sixth year in a row, so perhaps nobody takes me seriously anymore. But I see the quality of the work, the organization, and Mercedes. It has to work.

'If you had to say that the people were lazy, they are laid back, then you would have your doubts. But that is not the case. They are still performing to the same standard which has always been the McLaren trademark, in the way they operate and the quality of the work they turn out.'

This was how Keke Rosberg, ever the pragmatist, summed up the McLaren–Mercedes team's prospects for 1997. It was a crucial season, in which they would split with Marlboro, their title sponsors for more than 20 years, and forge a new deal with the German West cigarette brand.

The striking new McLaren–Mercedes MP4/12 was originally unveiled at breakfast time on Tuesday 14 January at the team's Woking factory, neatly decked out in the smart orange

livery which the team had first used in the 1960s. This was a
clever promotional device, enabling the new car to be shown
without taking the gloss off the lavish, multi-million-dollar
launch of the team's new sponsorship deal with West
cigarettes, staged at London's Alexandra Palace to the accom-
paniment of live entertainment from the Spice Girls and
Jamiroquai. The new McLaren had been completed just after
six o'clock in the morning of its preliminary unveiling. Four
hours later it was already being loaded into a transporter
which was shipped, together with its own tow van, direct
from Luton to Jeréz in a giant Ilyushin cargo jet in preparation
for David Coulthard's first test at the Spanish track.

The MP4/12 was a totally new machine with several
imaginative design innovations, as well as incorporating
features such as a rear impact zone, collapsible steering
column, reduced winglet area and suspension designed
within the limited aspect ratios designated by the new 1997
F1 technical regulations. It was powered by another new
Mercedes engine developed by Ilmor Engineering.

'This is another major evolution from the specification
which we used in the final race of last season,' explained Ilmor
boss Mario Illien. 'It involves a new block design which we
decided on for both performance and installation reasons.
The inlet system has been completely redesigned and it is also
marginally lighter. We have enhanced the power output, but
how much better it is in terms of driveability will only be
established once the car starts testing, although indications
from the dynamometer suggest that we have certainly made
improvements.'

From the outset, Ron Dennis was cautiously optimistic
about prospects for the new car, hinting that some significant

aerodynamic improvements had been found as a result of the intensive wind tunnel testing completed over the winter.

'We know that we have made quantifiable gains in the wind tunnel,' said Dennis, 'but I would be surprised if all the other teams haven't made corresponding improvements. The only thing we don't know is where they are starting from. That said, I think attempting to evaluate the qualities of the opposition is pretty much a waste of time. We just have to concentrate on developing the best car that we can.' Which they did.

Behind the scenes, Dennis was also taking additional decisive steps designed to strengthen the McLaren technical team. Towards the end of 1996 he had approached Williams's highly respected Chief Designer Adrian Newey with the offer of a job. Newey, widely regarded as being in a class of his own when it came to knowledge and understanding of Formula One aerodynamics, faced complications in terminating his Williams deal ahead of time. He was eventually to join the McLaren team in the middle of 1997. And he would contribute enormously to the restoration of their winning ways.

Meanwhile, pre-season testing proved very promising and Coulthard's run to victory in the first race of the season equally well merited, although admittedly made easier by the fact that both Williams drivers failed to complete the distance.

Coulthard not only won at Melbourne to cement the McLaren–Mercedes newly revived 'Silver Arrows' image, but backed that up with a second win at Monza before Häkkinen finally got his F1 victory tally off the mark at Jeréz.

There was a degree of inconsistency about the new McLaren's performances throughout the opening races of the season, but Häkkinen seemed more able to adapt his driving style to accommodate any incipient handling imbalance. By contrast, Coulthard struggled slightly if the car was not quite right, even though he racked up the hard results at a more rapid rate.

McLaren also displayed great resourcefulness when it came to planning its refuelling strategies. For example, at Buenos Aires, where the car proved not at its best in quali-fying trim on the harder of Goodyear's two tyre compounds, a one-stop strategy with a long opening stint helped translate Häkkinen's 17th place on the grid into fifth place at the chequered flag.

It was a strategy which worked well for the team again later in the year at Silverstone, although most outsiders believed that the McLaren management should have told a brake-troubled David Coulthard to move out of the path of his faster team-mate early in the race. Had it not been for the knock-on effect of a sticking wheel nut which caused Villeneuve's Williams to be stationary for 33.6 seconds at its first refuelling stop, Häkkinen would never have been in a position to surge through into the lead after Villeneuve made his second stop.

Nevertheless, once ahead, Häkkinen used the opportunity as a shop-window to display the full competitive edge of the McLaren–Mercedes wares, only for his hopes of victory to be cruelly dashed with engine failure only five laps from the finish line.

Objectively, McLaren should have won at least six Grands Prix during 1997. David Coulthard drove beautifully to post his second win of the season at Monza, slick pit work by the mechanics and the benefit of a larger fuel tank enabling him to vault ahead of Jean Alesi's Benetton come refuelling time. But McLaren should also have won at Montreal, Silverstone, Austria, the Nürburgring and, arguably, Suzuka, where Häkkinen was crucially wrong-footed by Eddie Irvine's Ferrari in the opening stages of the race.

Engine failures, including problems with oil system aeration and bottom-end defects, overshadowed the season. 'Although we had our share of engine failures, we won at Monza with the latest F-spec engine and might well have scored a 1–2 there without Mika's tyre problem,' said Norbert Haug, the Mercedes-Benz motorsport manager.

'We finished David in second place at Zeltweg after Mika stopped. You cannot say this is a complete 100 per cent unreliability problem, but we hope that we have now resolved these problems. But as far as our progress is concerned related to speed and lap times, this is quite promising and satisfying.

'But it is not so satisfying having all those near-misses and ending up with not enough victories. I am not satisfied with that, but the unreliability problems are sometimes the price you pay for an accelerated development programme designed to take you to the front of the field in the shortest possible time. Yet I think that we have proved that when the drivers have a competitive package, they can do a good job.'

As far as the 1998 driver line-up was concerned, McLaren opted for continuity and security by renewing its deals with Mika Häkkinen and David Coulthard. Ron Dennis wanted to see the two men who had shared the trials and tribulations involved in the team's renaissance finally share in the benefits.

In that connection, many F1 insiders believed Damon Hill should have bitten Dennis's hand off at the first hint of a possible deal. In 1997, McLaren re-established itself as a winning force. In 1998, they could well take over as F1's pace-setters.

Yet there had certainly been moments during the summer of 1997 when Häkkinen began to wonder if he would ever win a Grand Prix. The Hungarian race at Budapest was the 90th of his career, yet by then the 28-year old Finn had not only never won a race, he had never even started from pole position.

Despite this apparent performance shortfall, Häkkinen was still unquestionably regarded as a member of that exclusive coterie of 'ultimately fast' F1 competitors of the current generation. At Silverstone, of course, he came within 15 miles of winning the British Grand Prix before engine failure intervened. Jacques Villeneuve may have imagined that he was going to be able to overtake in the closing moments of the race. But Häkkinen just smiled indulgently when reflecting on the scenario.

'No way, not a chance,' he grins thinly. 'I absolutely had it all in hand. But I just could not believe it. Yet I thought, "What's the point of being upset?" I wasn't going to feel any better if I started throwing my helmet about the place. It won't help me, the engineers, the fans, so what's the point? So I decided to do the opposite – and I felt much better afterwards.'

One experienced insider likened Häkkinen to a bottle of champagne which has been given a vigorous shaking. 'He's like Ronnie Peterson when he went back to Lotus in 1978,' he noted. 'He's absolutely ready to deliver. Once he won his first Grand Prix, he could reel off a whole sequences of victories in quick succession.'

It was a scenario which clearly appealed to Mika. He is passionate in his enthusiasm and commitment to F1, yet still manages to conceal his ambition beneath a veneer of characteristically Scandinavian composure. When things went wrong, his face assumed an impassive, almost non-committal expression. When they went right, he allowed himself only the mildest impish smile.

Yet after two years with Lotus, a season as McLaren test driver and almost four full seasons in the Woking squad's race team, Häkkinen needed no reminding that time could be running out for his World Championship aspirations. So did he feel an air of frustration? And was he aware of approaching a crucial crossroads in his career?

'Ever since I joined McLaren in 1993, the whole process has been aimed towards winning,' he mused in measured tones.

'Since then we have spared nothing in our efforts to re-establish McLaren as the winning car. Now we are getting close to our target. Like we saw in Silverstone, like we saw with David [Coulthard] in Canada, like we saw with two podium finishes in Australia.

'So I think the word "frustration" is no longer the word we need to use any more. In truth, we must feel more motivated than ever because we are close to reaching our goal. And I do feel more motivated than ever – so hungry that it is unbelievable.'

So the special relationship with Ron Dennis and McLaren had not been damaged in any way by this apparently sustained shortage of results?

'Absolutely not,' he insisted. 'All these years we have been working together, Ron has shown himself to be enormously dedicated and committed, whether it be in his approach to his work or his family.

'He is always targeting excellence and asking a lot from the people he is working with. But he has always extremely supportive, whether in moments when the team has been strong or it has not been strong.'

Of course, continuity of engine supply is one matchless factor which contributes to long-term success in Formula One. Since splitting with Honda in 1992, McLaren had had a bumpy ride in this respect. Only since the start of 1995, with Mercedes-Benz, had there been a resumption of the sort of continuity which had served the Williams–Renault partnership so well for the entire decade. How challenging had this been to come to terms with from a driving standpoint?

'Yes, it has been difficult,' he said. 'But it is only technical stuff. For example, you say that 1994 was difficult. Yet if you look at the facts, I had a fantastic season. I scored six podiums. But on the other hand we had a lot of failures. Yet we went into the season knowing it was going to be a difficult year. It depends how you look on these things.

'It's not always a question of how many races you win, whether you scored three points or four points at this or that race. The real question is what are the lap times? Are they quickest, or not? If you are not quickest, you have a hell of a lot of work. If you are quickest, you still have a hell of a lot of work. We are now reaching the point when those times are very getting close indeed.

'Certainly I had some situations in 1996 when I was thinking that perhaps I shouldn't be so tired, I should be more fresh, and that this might have been a consequence of the accident.

'Yet the 100 per cent maximum commitment never left me. And I was supported flat-out by all the people around me. In such difficult conditions that support was mega-important. And I don't mean sympathy or pity. A kick in the bum sometimes, that's what you need.'

If you asked Mika whether he would like to change teams in 1998, his face would break into an almost foxy grin. No, he replied, he would like to stay with the McLaren–Mercedes alliance and finish the job he started at the end of 1993. 'I want to stay with McLaren,' he smiles. 'But if I *was* moving, I wouldn't tell you anyway!

'But if you look around the teams and consider how McLaren has been performing this season compared with previous years – both in terms of the development of car and engine – I would say that I do not want to change.'

# Chapter Six

# World Champion

Mika Häkkinen began the 1998 World Championship season as he meant to go on. By winning. He started the process at the beginning of March at the Australian Grand Prix, and by the time he took the chequered flag at Suzuka seven months later, he had won exactly half the season's 16 races to become only the second Finnish driver to take the title crown.

Yet from the outset, despite that maiden victory at Jeréz at the end of the previous season, Mika remained cautious in the extreme. He was upbeat, sure enough; but he had experienced too many false dawns during his F1 career to date to make too many over-optimistic predictions.

'Psychologically, winning your first Grand Prix makes a huge difference,' he conceded. 'It gives you a lot more confidence, makes you realize how easy winning really is. It makes you look at races differently, makes you more relaxed and takes off the pressure.

'It's flattering that there are people out there saying that David and myself are favourites for this year's World Championship, but Michael Schumacher is the best driver out there at the moment. You have to admit that, because you don't win two world titles by accident.

'It is not always a question of talent, it is how you use it. Michael has taken the best advantage out of himself and the car. But the knowledge and experience I have now should make me a more competitive driver than I was last year. We will just have to wait and see how it all unfolds.'

The acknowledgement that Schumacher was the best driver in the business opened up another fascinating chink of insight into Häkkinen's character. Those close to Mika recognized his own burning self-confidence. Inwardly, he had no doubt whatsoever that he could beat Michael in a straight fight. Yet his credentials – in terms of hard results – were so modest that to come out bragging that he could beat the German ace would have seemed strategically reckless. It would have dented Häkkinen's credibility at a crucial moment in his career when he stood poised to prove to the world that he had the talent to challenge Schumacher at the most exalted level. Best, under the circumstances, to let the performances out on track speak for themselves.

And they did. Throughout the 1998 season, Mika Häkkinen made few mistakes. He also handled the pressure of racing wheel-to-wheel with Michael Schumacher for the title crown. Put simply, the story of 1998 was Häkkinen's deft brilliance at the wheel of the strikingly liveried McLaren–Mercedes MP4/13, itself a steely symphony of cleverly blended grey and silver.

Having said this, the year began on a slightly uncomfortable note for Häkkinen when, due to a misunderstanding with his engineers, he mistakenly came into the pit lane during the course of the Australian Grand Prix. It was a slip which handed the lead to Coulthard, but the Scot was again requested to relinquish his advantage in line with a pre-race agreement between the two drivers that whichever of them reached the first corner ahead should win the race. And Häkkinen had done so.

This time, the Scot certainly gained himself the unstinting admiration of the F1 community by sticking to the terms of that pre-race pact, but the whole episode again raised lingering question marks over what should and should not be permissible in terms of team tactics.

The two men had agreed that whoever reached the first corner in the lead would take the win, assuming they had a clear-cut run at the front of the field without needing to fend off any outside opposition. Although Coulthard qualified second, he willingly agreed to the deal, believing that a track record of brilliant getaways stacked the odds strongly in his favour.

'Mika and I have learned a lot over the winter and are an awful lot closer together, and we agreed that whoever got to the first corner first, then we would not challenge the other,' said David. 'I think it was sensible under the circumstances as we had not done a full race distance prior to the race.

'I was very confident that I would beat Mika to the first corner, but Mika made the best start. I think he deserved to win the race, no question about it. I could think about it clearly and did what I thought was the right thing to do.'

As it was, Häkkinen went to dominate the race in flawless style, only losing the lead when a mix-up in the pits resulted in his being called in prematurely for his second refuelling stop with 22 of the race's 58 laps still to run. He was waved straight back into the race, returned to refuel four laps later and then resumed 33 seconds behind Coulthard.

The Scot duly made his second stop on lap 42, after which the two McLarens were left running in 1–2 formation 13.5

seconds apart. Häkkinen then produced a stunning demonstration of driving, rattling off a sequence of quick laps to pull up on to Coulthard's gearbox. With only two laps to go, Coulthard pulled over on the start/finish straight to honour his side of the agreement.

'What David did today was remarkable,' said Häkkinen after the race. 'I have been in F1 for many years and seen a great deal. It was really gentlemanly, unreal and fantastic.'

However, it was deeply questionable whether Coulthard should have been expected to abide by his agreement under these circumstances. Häkkinen's delay may have been the team's fault, but it was part of the natural ebb and flow of motor racing fortune. Correcting such a misfortune for the second successive race not only made Coulthard appear over-anxious to please, but arguably also devalued the quality of Häkkinen's victory.

Häkkinen's special relationship with McLaren was once more thrown into the spotlight during an incident which did not even involve him. This episode occurred at São Paulo's Interlagos circuit, the second round of the title chase.

After Coulthard had abandoned his McLaren MP4/13 out on the circuit following a spin, television cameras picked out an episode on the pit wall where the team's managing director Ron Dennis could clearly be seen admonishing the Scot for leaving the car where its technical details could be probed by prying photographers.

'In a nutshell, that's the difference,' said one McLaren insider. 'If Mika had done that, Ron would have never told him off in public in a million years!'

To be fair, Dennis later apologized to Coulthard. But the point seemed valid. Although McLaren were scrupulously

even-handed when it came to providing equality of equipment and technical support to their drivers, there was
certainly a personal relationship between Mika and the team
that Coulthard had yet to match.

To be at the wheel of a competitive car was a huge relief
for the lad from Helsinki. Going into battle at the wheel of an
uncompetitive machine had looked set to wear him down on
several occasions over the previous two or three years.

'It sometimes felt like an absolute disaster,' he remem-
bered. 'You put everything on the line, 100 per cent
commitment, to your life, your training, your efforts in qualifying and to race well. You know you have done everything
right, then you qualify ninth or tenth, and people just don't
understand.

'Even though you know in your own mind that you are a
good driver, if the car doesn't go quick enough, you just
cannot get the message over as to how much effort you are
putting into it. You have to explain to every single person just
what is involved.'

Now all that was all different. Just as Ron Dennis never
wavered in his belief that the McLaren–Mercedes partnership would eventually be established as a consistent winner,
so he always had faith that Häkkinen was capable of getting
the job done at the highest level.

So, was Mika developing a good relationship with David
Coulthard?

'I think so,' says Häkkinen. 'I think if I said a direct "Yes"
that would not be true. That's because team-mates are not
always best friends, and if they were it would not be good for
the team. There would not be that hunger for victory. So I
think we are friends, but not best friends.'

So, if push came to shove, would he sit it out with Coulthard in a head-to-head battle, even if it meant risking them both ending up in a gravel trap?

Häkkinen grinned with an almost compelling innocence. 'I really don't know,' he replied. Yet the expression on his face strongly suggested that he might well do just that.

Watching Häkkinen and Coulthard apparently toying with the opposition to win the Australian and Brazilian races at the start of the year, one could have been forgiven for thinking that the McLaren–Mercedes squad was destined to enjoy a season no more challenging than a brisk walk in the park. Yet nobody was under-estimating the opposition.

After a slow start, Michael Schumacher and the Ferrari team mounted a spectacular counter-attack. At the start of the year the Bridgestone-shod McLaren was overwhelmingly the best package in the business, but when Goodyear's development programme slipped into top gear it was clear that the McLaren drivers had a fight on their hands.

Those two wins at the start of the season gave Häkkinen a valuable cushion which would work in his favour. In the third race at Buenos Aires he was happy to take second to Michael Schumacher on a circuit the Finn does not particularly like.

Then came Imola, where David Coulthard scored his sole 1998 win of the season, a race in which Häkkinen stopped with gearbox failure. A rogue, counterfeit bearing had somehow found its way into the McLaren supply chain. Steps were taken to ensure it did not happen again.

The Spanish and Monaco Grands Prix produced brilliantly decisive wins for Häkkinen. They were significant because of the sheer high-speed precision he displayed on both occasions. Starting from pole position on both tracks, he vanquished the opposition to come away from the most glamorous race on the calendar with a 22-point lead over Schumacher.

By the time Mika was forging towards the 1998 World Championship title crown, he had developed the confident insouciance of a man who realizes his time has finally come. His victory in the '98 Spanish Grand Prix at Barcelona was possibly the Finn's finest performance yet, counfounding those critics who have said he is too dull and has not sufficient tactical ability to get the best out of any given strategic racing situation.

This reputation for not being the most interesting man around is not justified in Häkkinen's case. But it's easy to see how it has gained currency in journalistic circles. At F1 media conferences Mika's presence can be positively soporific. But if you have the opportunity of a one-to-one interview, he can be fascinating, dryly amusing and extremely perceptive.

Back-track for a moment to the circumstances behind Häkkinen's arrival at the start of 1993 and you'll quickly come to understand why the blond Finn has become McLaren's Favoured Baby. Whatever the management might say, there has often been an almost unconscious element of partiality in Häkkinen's favour.

Don't get me wrong. I'm not talking here about standards of car preparation or anything overt; simply personal chemistry. If David Coulthard sometimes looks slightly strained, betraying a feeling that perhaps he's regarded as the supporting cast, it's because of what Häkkinen has brought to McLaren over a much longer period.

Yet Häkkinen also showed his mettle when events were running against him during 1998. Both McLaren–Mercedes retired from the Canadian Grand Prix, Mika with gearbox problems at the start and David when he looked on course to beat Schumacher's Ferrari in a straight fight.

This could have been a crucial turning point, for by this time in the season any success which David achieved was increasingly being regarded as forming a safety net for Häkkinen's title hopes. Take points off Michael and you help Mika – even when Mika does not finish!

Ferrari's win at Montreal was the harbinger of three Schumacher victories off the reel. Mika had to settle for third in the French race at Magny-Cours behind a Ferrari 1–2, but he drove with great skill in a torrential downpour at Silverstone to lead the Ferrari number one at the height of the storm – only to slide off the road when the conditions became absolutely appalling.

Mika was lucky to find his way back on to the circuit after this excursion and, although he had damaged the McLaren's nose wings, it seemed that his 30-second lead over Schumacher would be sufficient to sustain his advantage. Unfortunately, the safety car was deployed to slow the field as the rain intensified and as a result that entire advantage evaporated. When the restart was given, those damaged nose wings meant that Mika was unable to keep the Ferrari ace back in second place.

After Silverstone, Schumacher had closed to within two points of Mika at the head of the championship table, but the Finn redressed the balance with two straight victories in the Austrian and German Grands Prix.

With 16 points in hand, Häkkinen headed into the Hungarian Grand Prix at Budapest in confident mood. He led from the start, only to be hampered by a front anti-roll bar working loose on his car, forcing him to slow his pace dramatically. Having had an easy win in his sights, he struggled home sixth after a brilliant performance of car conservation. And now he could seriously feel the pressure, with Michael closing to seven points behind.

The Belgian Grand Prix at Spa-Francorchamps effectively put the title chase on hold for one race. Neither Mika nor Michael made it to the finish. Häkkinen spun out on the first corner, his McLaren then rammed by Johnny Herbert's Sauber. For his part, Schumacher became involved in a controversial collision with David Coulthard's McLaren in torrential rain, the impact ripping off the Ferrari's right front wheel. Back in the pits an ugly scene threatened as Schumacher squared up to Coulthard, but the episode was defused largely thanks to Coulthard's calm and dignified attitude.

The Italian Grand Prix saw an emotional Ferrari 1–2, although the McLaren–Mercedes were certainly the faster cars on this occasion. Disappointingly, Coulthard's engine failed while he was leading, while a rare brake problem pitched Häkkinen into a 175 mph spin as he was closing on Schumacher in the second half of the race. In what McLaren boss Ron Dennis later described as 'the most heroic seven laps of the season,' Mika recovered to nurse his car home fourth with only the rear brakes working. It was a great display of damage limitation, but it meant that Mika and Michael left Monza sharing the title lead with 80 points apiece. The Championship could go either way.

Häkkinen now proved publicly that he had come of age. At the Luxembourg Grand Prix at the Nürburgring he spent the first 14 laps of the race boxed into third place behind Eddie

Irvine's Ferrari as Schumacher raced away into the distance. However, once second, Mika drove a simply stupendous race to emerge from his first refuelling stop ahead of Michael's Ferrari.

That gave Häkkinen the psychological edge. Five nail-biting weeks remained before the final race at Suzuka in Japan. Michael qualified the Ferrari on pole position, then stalled it at the start, a transgression which required him to start from the back of the grid. Mika had finally broken his challenge. Both men had withstood huge pressure, but at the end of the day it was Schumacher who had wobbled first.

Mika rounded off the season with another decisive win. The first to congratulate him at the finish was Schumacher, the Ferrari team leader having retired with a puncture while running third. 'He deserved it,' said Michael. 'He and his team were the best this year. But next season, I hope, it will be a different story.'

The man of the moment allowed himself a twinkle of a grin. As he waited with second and third placed Eddie Irvine and David Coulthard to go on to the victory rostrum, Ron Dennis looked at them all pleadingly. 'Please don't shower me with champagne,' he begged. 'It is just *so* cold.'

Häkkinen just winked at his employer. He at least knew the Finnish for 'no chance'. And he completed the job in the best traditions of Formula One.

In reflecting on Mika's first World Championship, the contribution of Mika's closest friend and confidante should never be ignored. After almost four years together, Mika and Erja Honkannen married in May 1998. Erja, an independent-minded, free-spirited and thoroughly sensible person, had helped nurse Mika through the delicate months following his accident at Adelaide in 1995.

Successfully playing the role of a Grand Prix driver's wife means mastering a complex balancing act. You need to be attentive without worrying, supportive without fussing. Erja seems to have managed this with considerable charm and good humour.

She is hugely popular among the McLaren team, who see her as an extremely positive influence on Mika throughout the year. She is interested in his job without being star-struck, displaying the inner confidence of somebody who has successfully developed her own career, in this case on Finnish television.

'Mika is a team worker,' she says in perceptive acknowledgement of her husband's professional qualities. 'He is not a guy who says "I did it" or "This is mine."

'He feels that it is important that everybody in the team understands him and he understands everybody else. I think that is his strength. He is not egocentric. People might think so, because he seems a bit closed, but it is not the case.'

She admits that the Adelaide accident had a profound effect on them both, as at that time she had only known him for about six months. 'It was quite traumatic,' she says. 'But I think that in this period Mika has learned a lot, not only about his job and everything to do with it, but also about life.

'We still talk about it sometimes. It gave him a sort of forced stop to think about things, to think about everything. It really made him stronger.'

Interestingly, Ron Dennis feels that his Scandinavian background was one of the crucial keys which helped Mika come to terms with the after-effects of the accident.

'You can't go through life and suffer those sort of experiences without them sitting in your mind somewhere,' he says.

'I think his ability to handle those thoughts is as much attributable to where he was born as anything else.

'I think Scandinavians have got a unique ability to lock things out of their minds and get on with life. Different countries and different cultures do have a direct bearing on the thought processes of people.'

Another key element buttressing the success of Häkkinen's racing career is the unobtrusive support he has received from Keke Rosberg. The senior Finn is always there to offer help off-stage, feeling no need of any self-promotion or publicity.

'I prefer to remain behind the scenes,' he said. 'I had all my attention when I was racing and now it is Mika's turn. I don't need it, I don't want it and just want to get on with my life.

'I no longer want to be in front of the camera. Now I prefer to be behind the camera, organizing the shoot.' It is a task which he and his colleague Didier Coton, the man who accompanies Mika to each and every race, carry out with meticulous and good-natured efficiency.

Predicting who would achieve what in the 1999 FIA Formula One World Championship looked like a substantially more difficult task than it had been in the previous few years. Obviously, everybody in the McLaren–Mercedes team had high hopes for the performance of their new car; but Häkkinen confessed he found himself more reluctant than usual to speculate just how everything would work out under the new tyre regulations which required an additional, fourth circumferential groove on the front covers.

'The fact that everybody will be running on Bridgestone tyres can also be expected to have a serious influence on the outcome of the new season,' said Mika.

'It is very difficult to judge whether the performance differentials between the various competing cars will be smaller or greater than we saw last year when Formula One was heavily involved in a tyre war between two manufacturers.

'There is also the issue of how the cars will handle on the four-grooved front tyres. I have heard a great deal of mixed comments from many of my colleagues on this topic, but I am determined not to pre-judge the situation and will be making my own personal conclusions once I have settled into the discipline of pre-season testing.

'Personally, I will be going back into action after the longest holiday away from the cockpit since I started my Grand Prix career. I have found this extremely positive because it has given me the opportunity to relax and recharge my motivation after that challenging and very satisfying 1998 season.

'As far as another World Championship is concerned, I feel more motivated than ever to win more races. I am sure David will be trying hard, but I'm afraid I won't be doing him any favours. I feel we start the year on an equal footing and I shall be trying to secure my second World Championship.'

As usual, the new McLaren–Mercedes MP4/14 was one of the last cars to be unveiled prior to the start of the new season, in line with long-established McLaren team tradition. 'I am hoping that the McLaren philosophy of maximizing the amount of development time and then building the car at the last possible moment will pay off again,' Mika continued.

'It would be all to easy to make a judgement that "Williams is going to do this" and "Ferrari is likely to do that," but the hard truth is that nobody is in a position to make a really accurate forecast. Clearly I have every confidence in both McLaren and Mercedes-Benz to get the very best out of the prevailing regulations – and obviously nobody can discount Michael Schumacher and Ferrari.

'When I clinched the World Championship at Suzuka last autumn, I made it clear that it was my ambition to retain the title in 1999. That still stands, but, equally, I am certain that there are plenty of others out there who would like to ensure a very different outcome to the new season!'

As things transpired, retaining his World Championship would turn out to be a desperately close call for Häkkinen, not least because defending Constructors' Champions McLaren had made a huge leap forward with the new MP4/14, paying for their technical audacity with a raft of early-season unreliability.

Powered by a lighter and lower 72-degree Mercedes F0110H V10 engine developing around 785 bhp at 16,700 rpm, the new car represented McLaren Technical Director Adrian Newey's formula to claw back some of the grip lost by the extra fourth groove now required in the front tyres by the revised technical rules.

With extra weight trimmed off the entire chassis/engine package, the new car had even more scope for strategic placement of ballast around the chassis. The new car was also more complex than its predecessor in the positioning of many of the car's ancillary components within the monocoque walls.

The MP4/14 was also not quite as user-friendly as its immediate predecessor, failing initially to instil its drivers with the same sense of confidence and 'chuckability'. On the limit, however, the new McLaren represented an appreciable step forward even though the more powerful Merc F0110H

V10 had rather less in the way of progressive power delivery than the 1998 engine.

One of the main issues which particularly affected McLaren – and most other cars, come to that – was the reduction in the front tyre contact patch caused by the introduction of a fourth circumferential groove. Complicating that issue, what came as something of a surprise was the reduction in rear grip produced by the latest generation of Bridgestone rubber.

This only became apparent during the early development of the MP4/14 after various fixed parameters of its design were established. This resulted in the need to alter the deployment of ballast around the car, but eventually everything was satisfactorily resolved in time for the opening race of the year.

Even so, assimilating all the lessons from the 1998 car and incorporating them into a ground-up re-design meant that McLaren ended up with too many risks in the design. It was a more complex approach which needed honing in the interests of reliability. And that process ate into too much of the season.

The partnership of Häkkinen and Coulthard continued for its fourth straight season, both drivers operating on identical contractual terms, according to which they were free to race for the World Championship until the management decided it was appropriate to call time and ask one to help the other. In this case it would be Coulthard being asked to help the reigning title holder; but by the time the McLaren management decided to intervene the team was boxed into a mathematical corner.

'New car' mechanical problems stopped both cars in the Australian Grand Prix; and while Häkkinen triumphed in

Brazil, it was only after a peculiar gear-change glitch dropped him to third place in the opening stages.

Make no mistake, at Interlagos Häkkinen comfortably had the legs of all his key rivals – with the exception of his luckless team-mate David Coulthard, who failed to finish after a gearbox failure rounded off a day which saw his engine stall on the grid and caused his brief, belated appearance in the race three laps behind the rest of the field. But, as Häkkinen accelerated through the gears down the hill away from the pits on lap four, to his horror, the McLaren MP4/14's seven-speed, semi-automatic sequential gearbox inexplicably missed the change from fifth to sixth.

'I thought the game was over,' said the incredulous Finn after the race. 'But I dropped down a gear, accelerated and it was all fine.' From then on there was no problem, but that fleeting setback dropped him back to third place behind Rubens Barrichello's brilliant Stewart and Schumacher's Ferrari. Now it was time to play the tactical card.

Coulthard again stopped with gearbox problems and did not get his points score off the deck until Imola, where he was roundly beaten into second place in the San Marino Grand Prix.

David still believes that his one-stop strategy would have been good enough to get the job done on that occasion, had it not been for the unfortunate intervention of many uncooperative backmarkers. It was a disappointment, but not as much as the outcome of the race for Häkkinen, who fell off in the early stages, pressing too hard in a vain attempt to prove that his two-stop strategy would leave him with the upper hand.

Monaco was a disaster for McLaren, possibly Häkkinen's worst race of the season. Beaten off pole, he eventually had to settle for a distant third place, unsettled and uncomfortable with the feel of his MP4/14. The car was subsequently checked over from end to end and no tangible mechanical defect was located.

Monaco also saw Schumacher begin what seemed at the time like a psychological battle against Häkkinen, referring – quite unjustifiably – to an incident during qualifying.

While on his pole position lap, Häkkinen passed a stationary yellow flag at Tabac where Hill had abandoned his Jordan with gearbox problems. From the start of that season the stationary yellow had ceased to be a valid signal – though nobody seemed to have told the marshals – but that didn't prevent Schumacher from trying, unsuccessfully, to whip up controversy over the incident, hinting that perhaps the flag was actually being waved. Which it was not.

Earlier Schumacher had also gestured in frustration to Pedro Diniz after the Sauber driver held up his Ferrari, sparking some vigorous comments from the German driver on the matter of blue overtaking flags.

'There is a rule that drivers and their teams must respect the blue flags,' he insisted. 'If they do not, morally we should see penalties. Nothing happened at Imola, so we hope that action will be taken here.'

The issue was in fact addressed at the drivers' briefing and the general verdict from the front runners after the race was that the slower cars had behaved very well when it came to neatly getting out of their way.

Häkkinen then won in Spain and Canada before everything started to unravel for him. He should have won at Magny-Cours had it not been for the team's surprising decision not to allow him out early in the rain-drenched qualifying session. He finally qualified 14th and finished second, despite a spin at a crucial moment.

That race saw Coulthard drive brilliantly in the opening stages, seizing the lead and pulling away strongly before electrical problems shut down his Merc V10. It was a performance which set the pleasant Scot up for a fine win on his home turf at Silverstone, this being a happy consolation prize after Häkkinen's car was withdrawn from the race after problems with the left rear wheel securing mechanism had earlier seen him shed a wheel out on the track.

Now came the sequence of bitter disappointment which could have cost Häkkinen his run at the title. The Austrian Grand Prix produced the lowest moment when Coulthard trapped the Finn into a second corner spin. David then didn't get sufficient assistance from the pits to evolve a winning strategy and the McLarens finished 2–3 behind Irvine's Ferrari, with a furious Häkkinen storming through to take the final place on the podium.

Despite the acute disappointment generated by this incident, no team orders for the rest of the 1999 season were imposed on the McLaren–Mercedes drivers. Not yet, at least.

McLaren was keeping its nerve. Ron Dennis vigorously rejected suggestions that it was time for Coulthard to accept a strategically deferential number two role to Häkkinen in order to protect the Finn's slender two-point lead at the head of the drivers' championship table.

'There is no question of that at the moment,' he said. 'It is far too early in the season to be considering such a strategy. We have the confidence to let both Mika and David get on with it.'

Ironically, in the past, Dennis's organization had ended up the beneficiary of a rival's reluctance to impose team orders on its drivers. In 1986, Williams drivers Nigel Mansell and Nelson Piquet raced each other for the world championship with the result that they took points off one another, diluting their individual achievement to the point where Alain Prost dodged through to win the championship at the last race. Driving a McLaren.

Dennis and his team knew at heart that the McLaren–Mercedes MP4/14 was a better car than its rival, the Ferrari F399, and that Häkkinen's climb back through the field in Austria further endorsed the Finn's status as possibly the best driver in the world.

Despite this, with nine out of 16 races completed, the victory tally was equal at 4–4 between McLaren and Ferrari, with Jordan the only interloper thanks to Heinz-Harald Frentzen's surprise victory in the French Grand Prix.

After the rostrum ceremony, Coulthard and Häkkinen disappeared into the Mercedes motorhome with team chief Ron Dennis, Mercedes motorsport director Norbert Haug and Jurgen Schrempp, the chairman of the huge Daimler–Chrysler combine which a fortnight earlier had agreed in principle to take a 40 per cent stake in the TAG McLaren group.

What was said behind closed doors was certainly not shared with the news-hungry media jostling around the paddock outside. However, it was established that Coulthard apologized to Häkkinen for his error, the World Champion accepted graciously and the two men agreed to put the incident behind them.

'Whatever happened on the second corner is no longer important,' said Häkkinen, 'and I appreciate David's apologies.

The car, however, did not feel right after the incident, but even so I just went flat out to regain positions and finish in the points.'

Having been through all this ten years earlier, when his cars driven by Ayrton Senna and Alain Prost had collided as they battled for the lead of the Japanese Grand Prix at Suzuka, Ron Dennis struck a philosophical chord as he reviewed the race.

'David hit some bad traffic for two or three laps before his pit stop,' he said, 'but we felt we had more than enough margin [to keep ahead].

'Then we had a throttle cut on David's car. It didn't cost him much in terms of track time, but it turned the engine off for about a second, and then he was a little cautious, just making sure that he didn't have a problem.

'The bottom line is that we could have cruised the race if it hadn't been for the incident. If you've got two competitive drivers in your team you've got a choice, and personally I think that the choice we make – which is to let the drivers race – is the right one.'

Tyre problems at Hockenheim then saw Mika crash out of the German Grand Prix, allowing Irvine to win again. McLaren reasserted itself with a fine 1–2 at Hungaroring, Coulthard following Häkkinen home after the Scot pressed Irvine into a mistake during the closing stages.

Then came another controversy. In the Belgian Grand Prix at Spa-Francorchamps, Coulthard beat Häkkinen off the line and the two cars rubbed wheels at the first corner, David staying ahead. Mika settled for second place and was hardly the happiest man in town, his discomfort heightened by the fact that Ron Dennis said that he'd been in the wrong as far as that first corner incident was concerned.

Häkkinen had qualified on pole position for the tenth time out of 11 races so far that season, but was slow off the mark after his McLaren crept slightly and he had to touch the brakes to avoid being penalized. Coulthard accelerated away down the outside from second place on the grid, then turned into the tight right-hand La Source hairpin where he inadvertently bumped Häkkinen's car.

'There has been criticism from some sections of the media when we re-signed David,' said Dennis robustly, 'and now he drives a superb race and there is criticism of our team tactics.

'The first corner incident was a close call, but David was clearly ahead before the braking point. Any change in the end position would have cost us our long-established reputation for dealing totally evenhandedly with our drivers.'

Many F1 insiders took the view that this was all very well, but Dennis risked his drivers racing each other out of the World Championship stakes with only three races left to run. They suggested that McLaren might live to regret not imposing team orders if Häkkinen, who admitted that he settled for second place at Spa after the first-corner episode, should fail to retain his title by a single point.

The result transformed Coulthard into a strong title contender with 46 points, only 14 behind Häkkinen, with four races and 40 points left to race for.

'I was in front going into the first corner,' he said, 'and it is very difficult to judge in your mirrors where your competitor is in those circumstances. I felt contact, moved away slightly to give Mika room and continued on my way.

'I am delighted to have finally won here at Spa which has always been my favourite track and a great challenge for every driver.'

Häkkinen, whose second place enabled him to scrape back into the lead of the World Championship by just a single point ahead of fourth place finisher Eddie Irvine, was less impressed. Having already lost those six points in Austria when Coulthard pushed him into a spin on the second corner of the race, he was not in a conciliatory mood when the two cars pulled into the paddock at the end of the race.

The two men stoically ignored each other after climbing from their silver McLarens and Häkkinen kept well out of the picture when it came to the ritual champagne-spraying on the victory rostrum.

'It was an experience again,' said the Finn, referring obliquely to their Austrian collision, 'and not a very pleasant one. No further comment, to be honest.'

It was one of the rare occasions when Häkkinen seemed to be cast in the role of McLaren outsider. His indignation was understandable. Notwithstanding the team's commitment to fair-handed treatment of its drivers, you could see he felt the same sort of indignation and bewilderment that Coulthard had experienced at Jeréz '97 and Melbourne '98.

Yet, for Mika, it was somehow even more difficult to come to terms with. Throughout the 1999 season he had been consistently the quicker McLaren driver and been let down by a succession of technical problems which had not been his fault. True enough, he'd crashed at Imola while leading. But that was a rare slip.

Under the circumstances, one could also understand Häkkinen's private belief that team orders should have been invoked in his favour on this day when the McLarens had a huge performance advantage. Coulthard might have deserved a fair crack at the title, but he hadn't been as quick as his team-mate over much of the season and Ferrari – McLaren's key rival – was adopting a very different strategy in backing Eddie Irvine, singularly and totally, in their quest for a drivers' championship crown.

Thereafter it seemed to be downhill all the way. Häkkinen, now frazzled, threw away a commanding lead at Monza in one of the most remarkable lapses of his career, blowing his hopes when he spun off and retired while running seven seconds ahead of Frentzen with 30 of the race's 53 laps completed.

It was an incomprehensible error on the part of the reigning World Champion and the second time during the 1999 season that he had thrown away an easy win, having crashed in identical circumstances during the San Marino Grand Prix at Imola. Unbelievably, Häkkinen selected first rather than second gear as he changed down under braking for the tight chicane beyond the Monza pits. The McLaren's rear wheels locked momentarily and he pirouetted gently to a halt on the gravel run-off area.

The emotion of the moment was all too much for the Finn, who had endured such a roller-coaster season of dramatically changing fortunes. He leaped from the car, threw away its steering wheel in acute frustration and hurled his gloves to the ground. A few moments later he could be seen crouched at the edge of the circuit, head bowed over his knees.

'I just couldn't believe it,' said Frentzen. 'Mika had a consistent seven-second lead in front of me. At the beginning I tried to keep up with him, but couldn't quite hold him. I was slightly worried about the very long opening stint [he refuelled on lap 35 of the 53 lap race] from the viewpoint of tyre wear, but once I was in the lead I was able to save the brakes, tyres and engine and just bring it home.'

From this point onwards it seemed as though Mika's fortunes were locked into a painful tailspin. Scrambled pit-stop strategy wrote him out of the equation in the European Grand Prix at the Nürburgring, where he was lucky to squeeze home fifth.

Then came the controversial Malaysian Grand Prix at Kuala Lumpur's dramatic new Sepang circuit. This was the race at which Häkkinen's arch-rival Michael Schumacher returned to the cockpit after recovering from the broken right leg he had sustained in the British Grand Prix at Silverstone.

Michael's involuntary removal from the World Championship equation had played into the hands of Häkkinen and McLaren. In theory, at least. Yet that mid-season run of disasters and disappointments prevented them from capitalizing on this advantageous situation. Now Michael was back, but this time pledged to assist Irvine in his quest for the drivers' title.

At Sepang, Schumacher shamelessly played the team card. After some initial grandstanding to remind the fans that he was the fastest man in the F1 business, Schumacher allowed Irvine to get ahead and win commandingly. For his part, Mika spent most of the race bottled up behind Michael who was back off the throttle – intermittently and unpredictably – in fast and medium-speed corners in an effort to unsettle Mika.

It worked. By the time Häkkinen climbed the steps to take third place on the rostrum alongside the two Ferrari drivers, he looked absolutely washed out. Now he would go into the final race on Japan's daunting Suzuka circuit four points behind Irvine. All the pressure was now bearing down on his shoulders.

And then it seemed to be lifted. Only hours after taking the chequered flag in Malaysia, the first and second place Ferraris were sensationally disqualified from the race after it was discovered that the aerodynamic deflectors positioned on either side of the chassis transgressed the rules. Häkkinen was proclaimed the winner. And World Champion for the second straight year.

Or was he? There was another unpredictable turn of events to follow. An FIA Court of Appeal hearing, convened in Paris on the Friday separating those two final races, reversed the exclusion decision. The Ferraris were reinstated to first and second places at Sepang. So Mika did, after all, head for Japan with everything to play for. Absolutely everything.

Häkkinen went on to acquit himself brilliantly in what was probably the most crucial single race of his entire career. He may have been outqualified to pole position by Schumacher, but when the starting signal was given, he surged into an immediate lead from second place on the starting grid.

Thereafter, the Flying Finn produced an impeccable performance to win the race commandingly for the second year in succession, earning himself a well-merited and glittering entry in the motor racing history books.

His achievement made him only the seventh driver in the 50-year history of the World Championship to have won back-to-back titles, an achievement previously achieved by Alberto Ascari, Juan Manuel Fangio, Jack Brabham, Alain Prost, Ayrton Senna and – perhaps most significantly – Michael Schumacher, the man he beat across the line here by just over five seconds.

Häkkinen also underlined another basic truth, namely that top sportsmen need other top sportsmen to compete against in order to keep them sharp. Just as the late Ayrton Senna admitted that he missed the stimulation of Alain Prost's rivalry when the Frenchman retired, so Häkkinen seems to have revitalized himself since Schumacher's return to the cockpit after the enforced layoff recovering from a broken leg.

Normally a reticent individual, Häkkinen could hardly contain himself. 'Brilliant,' he grinned. 'What a great British word to express how I feel. It was one of my best races and I shall never forget it. Thanks to everybody!'

In the McLaren camp there was much back-slapping among the mechanics and engineers, as well as philosophical commiserations with their opposite numbers in the Ferrari team. There may be tensions and rivalry between these two organizations at the upper level, but the foot soldiers who graft on the cars treat each other with well-merited mutual respect.

Mika Häkkinen had come through it all as an absolutely central plank of the McLaren team challenge. And Jo Ramirez is right when he says the Finn hasn't really changed. He still wanders the paddock with the slightly innocent look of a driver who can't quite believe that, after all these years, Formula One success has tapped him on the shoulder.

But it has assuredly done so. Champion of the world. Twice so, and going for a hat trick.

# Appendix

# Facts and figures

| | |
|---|---|
| Starts | 128 |
| Championships | 2 |
| Race wins | 14 |
| Pole positions | 21 |
| Fastest laps | 13 |
| Points | 294 |

*Information correct at the beginning of the 2000 season*

**1991**

| Pos | Race | Circuit | Entrant | Car/engine | Comment | Grid |
|---|---|---|---|---|---|---|
| Ret | United States | Phoenix | Team Lotus | 3.5 Lotus 102B-Judd V8 | Engine-oil union fire | 13 |
| 9 | Brazil | Interlagos | Team Lotus | 3.5 Lotus 102B-Judd V8 | 3 laps behind | 22 |
| 5 | San Marino | Imola | Team Lotus | 3.5 Lotus 102B-Judd V8 | 3 laps behind | 25 |
| Ret | Monaco | Monte Carlo | Team Lotus | 3.5 Lotus 102B-Judd V8 | Oil leak/caught fire | 26 |
| Ret | Canada | Montreal | Team Lotus | 3.5 Lotus 102B-Judd V8 | Spin | 24 |
| 9 | Mexico | Mexico City | Team Lotus | 3.5 Lotus 102B-Judd V8 | 2 laps behind | 24 |
| DNQ | France | Magny Cours | Team Lotus | 3.5 Lotus 102B-Judd V8 | | 27 |
| 12 | Great Britain | Silverstone | Team Lotus | 3.5 Lotus 102B-Judd V8 | 2 laps behind | 25 |
| Ret | Germany | Hockenheim | Team Lotus | 3.5 Lotus 102B-Judd V8 | Engine | 23 |
| 14 | Hungary | Hungaroring | Team Lotus | 3.5 Lotus 102B-Judd V8 | 3 laps behind | 26 |
| Ret | Belgium | Spa | Team Lotus | 3.5 Lotus 102B-Judd V8 | Engine | 24 |
| 14 | Italy | Monza | Team Lotus | 3.5 Lotus 102B-Judd V8 | 4 laps behind | 25 |
| 14 | Portugal | Estoril | Team Lotus | 3.5 Lotus 102B-Judd V8 | 3 laps behind | 26 |
| Ret | Spain | Barcelona | Team Lotus | 3.5 Lotus 102B-Judd V8 | Spin | 21 |
| Ret | Japan | Suzuka | Team Lotus | 3.5 Lotus 102B-Judd V8 | Spin | 21 |
| 19 | Australia | Adelaide | Team Lotus | 3.5 Lotus 102B-Judd V8 | Race stopped 14 laps | 25 |

## 1992

| Pos | Race | Circuit | Entrant | Car/engine | Comment | Grid |
|---|---|---|---|---|---|---|
| 9 | South Africa | Kyalami | Team Lotus | 3.5 Lotus 102D-Ford HB V8 | 2 laps behind | 21 |
| 6 | Mexico | Mexico City | Team Lotus | 3.5 Lotus 102D-Ford HB V8 | 1 lap behind | 18 |
| 10 | Brazil | Interlagos | Team Lotus | 3.5 Lotus 102D-Ford HB V8 | 4 laps behind | 24 |
| Ret | Spain | Barcelona | Team Lotus | 3.5 Lotus 102D-Ford HB V8 | Spin | 21 |
| DNQ | San Marino | Imola | Team Lotus | 3.5 Lotus 102D-Ford HB V8 | | 27 |
| Ret | Monaco | Monte Carlo | Team Lotus | 3.5 Lotus 107-Ford HB V8 | Clutch | 14 |
| DNS | " | " | Team Lotus | 3.5 Lotus 102D-Ford HB V8 | Practice only | - |
| Ret | Canada | Montreal | Team Lotus | 3.5 Lotus 107-Ford HB V8 | Gearbox | 10 |
| 4* | France | Magny Cours | Team Lotus | 3.5 Lotus 107-Ford HB V8 | *aggregate of 2 parts | 11 |
| 6 | Great Britain | Silverstone | Team Lotus | 3.5 Lotus 107-Ford HB V8 | | 9 |
| Ret | Germany | Hockenheim | Team Lotus | 3.5 Lotus 107-Ford HB V8 | Engine | 13 |
| 4 | Hungary | Hungaroring | Team Lotus | 3.5 Lotus 107-Ford HB V8 | | 16 |
| 6 | Belgium | Spa | Team Lotus | 3.5 Lotus 107-Ford HB V8 | | 8 |
| Ret | Italy | Monza | Team Lotus | 3.5 Lotus 107-Ford HB V8 | Electrics | 11 |
| 5 | Portugal | Estoril | Team Lotus | 3.5 Lotus 107-Ford HB V8 | 1 lap behind | 7 |
| Ret | Japan | Suzuka | Team Lotus | 3.5 Lotus 107-Ford HB V8 | Engine | 7 |
| 7 | Australia | Adelaide | Team Lotus | 3.5 Lotus 107-Ford HB V8 | 1 lap behind | 10 |

## 1993

| Pos | Race | Circuit | Entrant | Car/engine | Comment | Grid |
|---|---|---|---|---|---|---|
| Ret | Portugal | Estoril | Marlboro McLaren | 3.5 McLaren MP4/8-Ford HB V8 | Accident | 3 |
| 3 | Japan | Suzuka | Marlboro McLaren | 3.5 McLaren MP4/8-Ford HB V8 | | 3 |
| Ret | Australia | Adelaide | Marlboro McLaren | 3.5 McLaren MP4/8-Ford HB V8 | Brakes | 5 |

## 1994

| Pos | Race | Circuit | Entrant | Car/engine | Comment | Grid |
|---|---|---|---|---|---|---|
| Ret | Brazil | Interlagos | Marlboro McLaren Peugeot | 3.5 McLaren MP4/9-Peugeot V10 | Engine/electrics | 8 |
| Ret | Pacific | T. I. Circuit | Marlboro McLaren Peugeot | 3.5 McLaren MP4/9-Peugeot V10 | Hydraulics | 4 |
| 3 | San Marino | Imola | Marlboro McLaren Peugeot | 3.5 McLaren MP4/9-Peugeot V10 | | 8 |
| Ret | Monaco | Monte Carlo | Marlboro McLaren Peugeot | 3.5 McLaren MP4/9-Peugeot V10 | Accident | 2 |
| Ret | Spain | Barcelona | Marlboro McLaren Peugeot | 3.5 McLaren MP4/9-Peugeot V10 | Engine | 3 |
| Ret | Canada | Montreal | Marlboro McLaren Peugeot | 3.5 McLaren MP4/9-Peugeot V10 | Engine | 7 |
| Ret | France | Magny Cours | Marlboro McLaren Peugeot | 3.5 McLaren MP4/9-Peugeot V10 | Engine | 9 |
| 3* | Great Britain | Silverstone | Marlboro McLaren Peugeot | 3.5 McLaren MP4/9-Peugeot V10 | *2nd place DSQ | 5 |
| Ret | Germany | Hockenheim | Marlboro McLaren Peugeot | 3.5 McLaren MP4/9-Peugeot V10 | Accident | 8 |
| 2* | Belgium | Spa | Marlboro McLaren Peugeot | 3.5 McLaren MP4/9-Peugeot V10 | *1st place DSQ | 8 |
| 3 | Italy | Monza | Marlboro McLaren Peugeot | 3.5 McLaren MP4/9-Peugeot V10 | | 7 |
| 3 | Portugal | Estoril | Marlboro McLaren Peugeot | 3.5 McLaren MP4/9-Peugeot V10 | | 4 |
| 3 | Europe | Jerez | Marlboro McLaren Peugeot | 3.5 McLaren MP4/9-Peugeot V10 | | 9 |
| 7 | Japan | Suzuka | Marlboro McLaren Peugeot | 3.5 McLaren MP4/9-Peugeot V10 | | 8 |
| 12 | Australia | Adelaide | Marlboro McLaren Peugeot | 3.5 McLaren MP4/9-Peugeot V10 | Accident | 4 |

**1995**

| Pos | Race | Circuit | Entrant | Car/engine | Comment | Grid |
|---|---|---|---|---|---|---|
| 4 | Brazil | Interlagos | Marlboro McLaren Mercedes | 3.0 McLaren MP4/10-Mercedes V10 | 1 lap down | 7 |
| Ret | Argentina | Buenos Aires | Marlboro McLaren Mercedes | 3.0 McLaren MP4/10-Mercedes V10 | Accident | 5 |
| 5 | San Marino | Imola | Marlboro McLaren Mercedes | 3.0 McLaren MP4/10-Mercedes V10 | 1 lap down | 6 |
| Ret | Spain | Barcelona | Marlboro McLaren Mercedes | 3.0 McLaren MP4/10-Mercedes V10 | Fuel pressure | 9 |
| Ret | Monaco | Monte Carlo | Marlboro McLaren Mercedes | 3.0 McLaren MP4/10B-Mercedes V10 | Engine | 6 |
| Ret | Canada | Montreal | Marlboro McLaren Mercedes | 3.0 McLaren MP4/10B-Mercedes V10 | Accident | 7 |
| 7 | France | Magny Cours | Marlboro McLaren Mercedes | 3.0 McLaren MP4/10B-Mercedes V10 | 1 lap down | 8 |
| Ret | Great Britain | Silverstone | Marlboro McLaren Mercedes | 3.0 McLaren MP4/10B-Mercedes V10 | Electrics | 8 |
| Ret | Germany | Hockenheim | Marlboro McLaren Mercedes | 3.0 McLaren MP4/10B-Mercedes V10 | Engine | 7 |
| Ret | Hungary | Hungaroring | Marlboro McLaren Mercedes | 3.0 McLaren MP4/10B-Mercedes V10 | Engine | 5 |
| Ret | Belgium | Spa | Marlboro McLaren Mercedes | 3.0 McLaren MP4/10B-Mercedes V10 | Spin | 3 |
| 2 | Italy | Monza | Marlboro McLaren Mercedes | 3.0 McLaren MP4/10B-Mercedes V10 | | 7 |
| Ret | Portugal | Estoril | Marlboro McLaren Mercedes | 3.0 McLaren MP4/10B-Mercedes V10 | Engine | - |
| DNS | | | Marlboro McLaren Mercedes | 3.0 McLaren MP4/10B-Mercedes V10 | Practice only | 13 |
| 8 | Europe | Nürburgring | Marlboro McLaren Mercedes | 3.0 McLaren MP4/10B-Mercedes V10 | 2 laps down | 9 |
| 2 | Japan | Suzuka | Marlboro McLaren Mercedes | 3.0 McLaren MP4/10B-Mercedes V10 | | 3 |
| DNS | Australia | Adelaide | Marlboro McLaren Mercedes | 3.0 McLaren MP4/10B-Mercedes V10 | Practice accident | (24) |

## 1996

| Pos | Race | Circuit | Entrant | Car/engine | Comment | Grid |
|---|---|---|---|---|---|---|
| 5 | Australia | Melbourne | Marlboro McLaren Mercedes | McLaren MP4/11-Mercedes V10 | | 5 |
| 4 | Brazil | Interlagos | Marlboro McLaren Mercedes | McLaren MP4/11-Mercedes V10 | 1 lap down | 7 |
| Ret | Argentina | Buenos Aires | Marlboro McLaren Mercedes | McLaren MP4/11-Mercedes V10 | Throttle | 8 |
| 8 | Europe | Nürburgring | Marlboro McLaren Mercedes | McLaren MP4/11-Mercedes V10 | | 9 |
| 8 | San Marino | Imola | Marlboro McLaren Mercedes | McLaren MP4/11-Mercedes V10 | 2 laps down | 11 |
| 6 | Monaco | Monte Carlo | Marlboro McLaren Mercedes | McLaren MP4/11-Mercedes V10 | 5 laps down | 8 |
| 5 | Spain | Catalunya | Marlboro McLaren Mercedes | McLaren MP4/11-Mercedes V10 | 1 lap down | 10 |
| 5 | Canada | Montreal | Marlboro McLaren Mercedes | McLaren MP4/11-Mercedes V10 | 1 lap down | 6 |
| 5 | France | Magny-Cours | Marlboro McLaren Mercedes | McLaren MP4/11-Mercedes V10 | | 5 |
| 3 | Great Britain | Silverstone | Marlboro McLaren Mercedes | McLaren MP4/11-Mercedes V10 | | 4 |
| Ret | Germany | Hockenheim | Marlboro McLaren Mercedes | McLaren MP4/11-Mercedes V10 | Gearbox | 4 |
| 4 | Hungary | Hungaroring | Marlboro McLaren Mercedes | McLaren MP4/11-Mercedes V10 | 1 lap down | 7 |
| 3 | Belgium | Spa | Marlboro McLaren Mercedes | McLaren MP4/11-Mercedes V10 | | 6 |
| 3 | Italy | Monza | Marlboro McLaren Mercedes | McLaren MP4/11-Mercedes V10 | | 4 |
| Ret | Portugal | Estoril | Marlboro McLaren Mercedes | McLaren MP4/11-Mercedes V10 | Accident | 7 |
| 3 | Japan | Suzuka | Marlboro McLaren Mercedes | McLaren MP4/11-Mercedes V10 | | 5 |

## 1997

| Pos | Race | Circuit | Entrant | Car/engine | Comment | Grid |
| --- | --- | --- | --- | --- | --- | --- |
| 3 | Australia | Melbourne | West McLaren Mercedes | McLaren MP4/12-Mercedes V10 | | 6 |
| 4 | Brazil | Interlagos | West McLaren Mercedes | McLaren MP4/12-Mercedes V10 | | 4 |
| 5 | Argentina | Buenos Aires | West McLaren Mercedes | McLaren MP4/12-Mercedes V10 | | 17 |
| 6 | San Marino | Imola | West McLaren Mercedes | McLaren MP4/12-Mercedes V10 | 1 lap down | 8 |
| Ret | Monaco | Monte Carlo | West McLaren Mercedes | McLaren MP4/12-Mercedes V10 | Accident | 8 |
| 7 | Spain | Barcelona | West McLaren Mercedes | McLaren MP4/12-Mercedes V10 | | 5 |
| Ret | Canada | Montreal | West McLaren Mercedes | McLaren MP4/12-Mercedes V10 | Accident | 9 |
| Ret | France | Magny-Cours | West McLaren Mercedes | McLaren MP4/12-Mercedes V10 | Engine | 10 |
| Ret | Great Britain | Silverstone | West McLaren Mercedes | McLaren MP4/12-Mercedes V10 | Engine | 3 |
| 3 | Germany | Hockenheim | West McLaren Mercedes | McLaren MP4/12-Mercedes V10 | | 3 |
| Ret | Hungary | Hungaroring | West McLaren Mercedes | McLaren MP4/12-Mercedes V10 | Hydraulics | 4 |
| DSQ | Belgium | Spa | West McLaren Mercedes | McLaren MP4/12-Mercedes V10 | Fuel irregularity | 5 |
| 9 | Italy | Monza | West McLaren Mercedes | McLaren MP4/12-Mercedes V10 | | 5 |
| Ret | Austria | A1-Ring | West McLaren Mercedes | McLaren MP4/12-Mercedes V10 | Engine | 2 |
| Ret | Luxembourg | Nürburgring | West McLaren Mercedes | McLaren MP4/12-Mercedes V10 | Engine | 1 |
| 4 | Japan | Suzuka | West McLaren Mercedes | McLaren MP4/12-Mercedes V10 | | 4 |
| 1 | Europe | Jerez | West McLaren Mercedes | McLaren MP4/12-Mercedes V10 | | 5 |

## 1998 (World Champion)

| Pos | Race | Circuit | Entrant | Car/engine | Comment | Grid |
|-----|------|---------|---------|------------|---------|------|
| 1 | Australia | Melbourne | West McLaren Mercedes | McLaren MP4/13-Mercedes V10 | | 1 |
| 1 | Brazil | Interlagos | West McLaren Mercedes | McLaren MP4/13-Mercedes V10 | | 1 |
| 2 | Argentina | Buenos Aires | West McLaren Mercedes | McLaren MP4/13-Mercedes V10 | | 3 |
| Ret | San Marino | Imola | West McLaren Mercedes | McLaren MP4/13-Mercedes V10 | Gearbox | 2 |
| 1 | Spain | Barcelona | West McLaren Mercedes | McLaren MP4/13-Mercedes V10 | | 1 |
| 1 | Monaco | Monte Carlo | West McLaren Mercedes | McLaren MP4/13-Mercedes V10 | | 1 |
| Ret | Canada | Montreal | West McLaren Mercedes | McLaren MP4/13-Mercedes V10 | Gearbox | 2 |
| 3 | France | Magny-Cours | West McLaren Mercedes | McLaren MP4/13-Mercedes V10 | | 1 |
| 2 | Great Britain | Silverstone | West McLaren Mercedes | McLaren MP4/13-Mercedes V10 | | 1 |
| 1 | Austria | A1-Ring | West McLaren Mercedes | McLaren MP4/13-Mercedes V10 | | 3 |
| 1 | Germany | Hockenheim | West McLaren Mercedes | McLaren MP4/13-Mercedes V10 | | 1 |
| 6 | Hungary | Hungaroring | West McLaren Mercedes | McLaren MP4/13-Mercedes V10 | 1 lap down | 1 |
| Ret | Belgium | Spa | West McLaren Mercedes | McLaren MP4/13-Mercedes V10 | Accident | 1 |
| 4 | Italy | Monza | West McLaren Mercedes | McLaren MP4/13-Mercedes V10 | | 3 |
| 1 | Luxembourg | Nürburgring | West McLaren Mercedes | McLaren MP4/13-Mercedes V10 | | 3 |
| 1 | Japan | Suzuka | West McLaren Mercedes | McLaren MP4/13-Mercedes V10 | | 2 |

## 1999 (World Champion)

| Pos | Race | Circuit | Entrant | Car/engine | Comment | Grid |
|-----|------|---------|---------|------------|---------|------|
| Ret | Australia | Melbourne | West McLaren Mercedes | McLaren MP4/14-Mercedes V10 | Throttle | 1 |
| 1 | Brazil | Interlagos | West McLaren Mercedes | McLaren MP4/14-Mercedes V10 | | 1 |
| Ret | San Marino | Imola | West McLaren Mercedes | McLaren MP4/14-Mercedes V10 | Accident | 1 |
| 3 | Monaco | Monte Carlo | West McLaren Mercedes | McLaren MP4/14-Mercedes V10 | | 1 |
| 1 | Spain | Barcelona | West McLaren Mercedes | McLaren MP4/14-Mercedes V10 | | 1 |
| 1 | Canada | Montreal | West McLaren Mercedes | McLaren MP4/14-Mercedes V10 | | 2 |
| 2 | France | Magny-Cours | West McLaren Mercedes | McLaren MP4/14-Mercedes V10 | | 14 |
| Ret | Great Britain | Silverstone | West McLaren Mercedes | McLaren MP4/14-Mercedes V10 | Wheel hub | 1 |
| 3 | Austria | A1-Ring | West McLaren Mercedes | McLaren MP4/14-Mercedes V10 | | 1 |
| Ret | Germany | Hockenheim | West McLaren Mercedes | McLaren MP4/14-Mercedes V10 | Accident | 1 |
| 1 | Hungary | Hungaroring | West McLaren Mercedes | McLaren MP4/14-Mercedes V10 | | 1 |
| 2 | Belgium | Spa | West McLaren Mercedes | McLaren MP4/14-Mercedes V10 | | 1 |
| Ret | Italy | Monza | West McLaren Mercedes | McLaren MP4/14-Mercedes V10 | Spin | 1 |
| 5 | Europe | Nürburgring | West McLaren Mercedes | McLaren MP4/14-Mercedes V10 | | 3 |
| 3 | Malaysia | Sepang | West McLaren Mercedes | McLaren MP4/14-Mercedes V10 | | 4 |
| 1 | Japan | Suzuka | West McLaren Mercedes | McLaren MP4/14-Mercedes V10 | | 2 |

# Q

# Other motor sport books from Queensgate Publications

### Track Record   Maurice Rowe   1-902655-00-1

The photography of *The Motor* magazine's former Chief Photographer, Maurice Rowe. Over 300 black and white and colour images from F1 and sports cars, 1950-1980.

### Racers 1948-1968   Doug Nye   1-902655-01-X

Part One of two volumes celebrating the greatest drivers in F1. Doug Nye selects his Top 20, from Wimille to Hulme. Lavishly illustrated with over 250 photographs.

### Racers 1969-2000   Alan Henry   1-902655-028

Part Two of the *Racers* series, celebrating the modern era of Grand Prix. *Autocar*'s long-time correspondent profiles his star drivers from Jochen Rindt to Mika Häkkinen.

### Schumi   Alan Henry   1-902655-27-3

Alan Henry profiles the world's leading racing driver and examines his Grand Prix career to date, including his controversial return from 'that' Silverstone accident.

**The Grand Prix Bible   Mike Lawrence   1-902655-25-7**

Encyclopaedic facts and figures guide to Formula 1. Driver histories, race facts, circuit details, technical information: this is the ultimate armchair guide.

## Also from Queensgate Publications

**Golf: A Mind Game**   Butler/Galvin   1-902655-03-6
**Action Guide Europe**   Watkins/Grogan   1-902655-06-0

**Queensgate** is distributed in the UK by

MDL Sales
Macmillan Distribution Ltd
Brunel Road
Houndmills
Basingstoke
Hants RG21 6XS

Tel 01256 302775
Fax 01256 351437

**Queensgate** is distributed in the USA by

Trafalgar Square Publishing
PO Box 257
Howe Hill Road
North Pomfret
Vermont 05053

Tel 802 457 1911
Fax 802 457 1913
www.trafalgarsquarebooks.com